10-5-60                                          B

D0463770

*Learn More with Less Effort*

Under the Editorship of

Gardner Murphy

# *Learn* MORE
# WITH LESS EFFORT

*by*
*George J. Dudycha*

PROFESSOR OF PSYCHOLOGY
WITTENBERG COLLEGE

HARPER & BROTHERS, PUBLISHERS
NEW YORK

Library of Congress catalog card number: 57–9868

Dedicated to

**Carol Ann**
and
**Arthur Lynn**

# Contents

# Preface

THIS BOOK is addressed primarily to college students, but all adolescents and adults who are interested in increasing the efficiency and effectiveness of their learning will find it a useful guide. Its contents deal chiefly with attitudes and techniques. The first two chapters are designed to aid the student to gain insight into his attitudes toward learning and to analyze the nature of his motivation. Chapter 3 gives the reader an understanding of the nature of the learning process and thus prepares him for a keener appreciation of the psychological significance of the learning techniques presented in the next three chapters. Chapter 7 discusses the attitudes and techniques that are effective in classroom learning and the next chapter deals with the physical surroundings that facilitate or hinder learning. The last chapter shows the student how to prepare for and to write examinations so that he can communicate effectively that which he has learned.

I am indebted to Dr. Gardner Murphy for his careful reading of the manuscript, to the artist who transformed my crude sketches into finished drawings, and to the various authors, editors, and publishers who have given their permission to use previously published materials. I am most grateful to my wife, Martha M. Dudycha, for her critical

examination of the manuscript and for her painstaking reading of the proofs. Without her assistance this book would not
have been brought to completion.

GEORGE J. DUDYCHA

*Springfield, Ohio*
*May 30, 1957*

*Learn More with Less Effort*

# 1.

# An Analysis of Our Psychology

## EFFICIENCY WINS!

EFFICIENCY is characteristically American. As Americans we pride ourselves on our ability to make things bigger and better and faster and in larger quantities than anyone else. The goal of every American industry is to produce a superior product in less time and at lower cost than that produced by its competitors. In war, this industrial efficiency helped us win; in peace, it helps us maintain a high standard of living.

Efficiency is not confined to industry alone. We find it in other areas of life as well. Your championship basketball team or football team, for instance, placed first in the conference because of individual skill and group efficiency. They won because each player did the right thing and at the right time with a minimum of lost motion and a minimum of wasted effort. This efficiency we call "teamwork." No one needs to tell us that this efficient teamwork pays dividends on the scoreboard.

Individual efficiency is teamwork within the individual. An efficient worker, an efficient player, or an efficient student

## YOU MAY BE A SKILLED

PITCHER

BALLET DANCER

TYPIST

## ARE YOU A SKILLED

LEARNER ?

FIGURE 1. Each Skill Must Be Established with Care, Purpose, and Effort.

is efficient because he accomplishes the most with the expenditure of the least amount of time and the least amount of effort. This economy of time and energy that we call efficiency is due to right habits firmly established. This fact you must note. The secret of efficiency is *correct habits firmly fixed.*

Without a doubt you do possess many efficient habits that you have established in the past. Perhaps you can throw a curved ball exceptionally well; or you can type with speed and accuracy; or you are a skilled ballet dancer. Because you can throw a curved ball, however, does not mean that you are a skilled typist or a ballet dancer. Each of these skills is very different from the others and each is learned only after prolonged practice. This you accept as a very obvious fact. Obvious as this fact is, however, many people, perhaps you included, fail to recognize that *each skill* must be established separately with care, purpose, and effort.

Let us take your study habits as an instance. Are they efficient? They are not apt to be unless you have spent time thinking about them and effort in improving them. Remember, you didn't just happen to throw curved balls or turn graceful cartwheels. You learned these skills only after practice. The same is true for all of your skills. Study habits are no exception to this rule. You must *learn* to study efficiently!

## AN OLD STORY

You probably have been told, not once but many times, *what to do* and *what not to do* when studying. Both your teachers and your parents have dinned do's and don't's into your ears until you have felt like screaming. Somewhere in your high-school career, perhaps in your Social Living course, you have discussed good and bad study habits, and some of your teachers may have even forced you to read one or more books on the subject and to write a report based on your reading. You have talked about studying both in and out of the classroom, with teachers, parents and teen-aged friends until you are weary of the whole subject. So, somewhat resignedly, you are thinking: *This is certainly no new topic!*

## THE NEW LOOK

You are right! This is not a new topic. Nevertheless, let us see whether we can take a new look at this old problem of learning.

Have you ever had the experience of seeing an old and very familiar object or situation in an entirely new way? I am certain that you have. Take that dress which your girl friend has worn on several dates and which you saw each time as so many navy blue blobs on a cream-colored background, and which came alive last night when you noticed for the first time that the blue blobs really were Mexican hats scattered in all kinds of positions on a light background. From that moment on the dress has had a new meaning for you—you had *a new look* at it. No longer is it a speckled blue haze; now it is "the Mexican-hat dress." It has a new meaning for you now. Your point of view is different. Anything can take on new meaning and significance, just as that dress did, when we change our point of view—when we see things from a new vantage point.

Do you remember that piece of driftwood that you stumbled over when you made your dash across the beach last summer for your first plunge into the lake? At the lake you saw that driftwood as an unnecessary and frustrating obstruction that interfered with your dash down the beach. Someone with imagination picked up that piece of driftwood and brought it home, where you see it today, also with imagination, as some prehistoric monster ready to spring. That piece of driftwood has changed from an annoying obstruction to a thing of beauty, to something that you enjoy because you have taken *a new look* at it. Even an old,

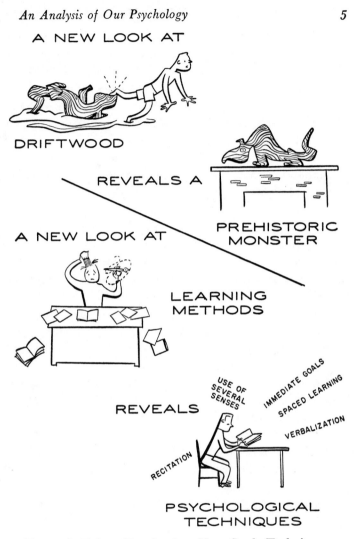

A NEW LOOK AT

DRIFTWOOD

REVEALS A

PREHISTORIC MONSTER

A NEW LOOK AT

LEARNING METHODS

REVEALS

USE OF SEVERAL SENSES

IMMEDIATE GOALS

SPACED LEARNING

VERBALIZATION

RECITATION

PSYCHOLOGICAL TECHNIQUES

FIGURE 2. Take a New Look at Your Study Techniques.

well-worn comic book that you have read again and again can stimulate new interest if you pick it up today and look

at it from the standpoint of the cartoonist's composition—
the way in which the comic characters are drawn. Now the
old comic book looks different because you have changed
your point of view. You are taking *a new look* at it!

What are we trying to say? Simply this: Our interest in
something, the meaning and the significance that it has for
us, *depends on us*. It depends on our mental set. As someone
once said: "We see things not as they are but as we are."
With this in mind, let us examine our mental set toward study
habits and toward learning.

## A COMMON ATTITUDE

It is quite likely that you agreed when we pointed out
above that all this talk about study procedures and study habits is "old stuff." Just why are we quick to label anything that
has to do with effective learning as old stuff? There are several reasons for this and not all are true for each of us.

For one thing, book learning is difficult for many people.
To learn something new that involves ideas, many of us have
to work at it. This is frustrating and annoying. As children
we had simple wants that could be satisfied easily and quickly.
When we indicated that we were hungry, we were fed. When
we wanted to climb up on mother's lap, she helped us up;
and when three seconds later we wanted to get down, she
helped us down. Our wants then were quickly satisfied often
with little effort on our own part. Therefore, we were quite
constantly experiencing the joy of satisfaction. It is this
achievement of our goals, and the consequent release from
tension, that is satisfying.

As we grow older, enter adolescence, and approach maturity, some of our goals, and certainly many of our tasks,
are set by someone else. Many of these goals are not easily
achieved, nor are the tasks as quickly and easily accomplished

as those in our early childhood. Since they take longer, satisfaction is postponed, tension is sustained and sometimes even increased. This is unpleasant and hence we generally refer to any activity of this type as *work*.

School subjects are particularly of this type. They consist of tasks assigned by teachers that require much time and hence postpone achievement, completion, and release. Solving a series of knotty algebra problems may require several hours of time which, if not spent, results in partial or even total failure. Thus, if one does or doesn't work at the assignment, either may be tension provoking. The same is true of translating a difficult passage of Latin, writing an acceptable composition, or finding an unknown in chemistry. Because we put our stress on the *completion* of assignments, rather than on the *process of achieving* our goals, which are often remote and sometimes actually not achievable, we refer to the tasks involved in school subjects as work. Our whole psychology is to rid ourselves of this and to experience uninhibited pleasure—to have constantly the joy of completion and achievement.

Therefore, when a school counselor, teacher, or parent suggests to you some method by which more learning can be accomplished, you may react to it as a device that will force you, rather than enable you, to do *more work* when work is the very thing you are trying to rid yourself of. You resent these efforts on the part of adults to change your study habits.

## OUR REACTION TO CHANGE

When we don't like something, we are apt to call it some name that sounds uncomplimentary. This is why the "old stuff" label, referred to above, seems so appropriate. The negative response to efforts to improve study habits is born of the

# OLD HABITS PERSIST

# EVEN THOUGH NEW HABITS

# MAY MAKE LIFE EASIER

FIGURE 3. Are You as Unwilling to Change Your Study
Habits as the Chinese Coolies Were to Stop Carrying
Heavy Loads on Their Heads?

fear that any improvement in efficiency will result only in more work which is necessarily disagreeable. This reasoning is entirely false. Efficient study techniques decrease frustration and tension and actually increase the satisfaction and pleasantness that one naturally seeks.

There is another aspect to this psychology of not accepting enthusiastically new approaches to learning, namely, adopting new approaches to learning necessitates change, adaptation, and readjustment. This is seldom easy and many people have a tendency to resist change. They prefer to remain in the old groove rather than learn a new way of doing things, even though the new way is much easier and more efficient.

An American businessman once observed a group of Chinese coolies unloading cargo, consisting of large and heavy boxes, from a ship. As was their custom, the coolies carried the heavy boxes on their heads. Seeking to help the coolies conserve their energy, the businessman provided each one with a two-wheeled truck on which to haul the boxes. Later, when he returned to see how much the coolies were enjoying the new trucks he had provided, he was amazed to find that each coolie was now carrying *both* the truck and the box on his head. They had carried cargo on their heads so long that they could not conceive of doing it any other way, even though the new way would be much easier. Are not we like the Chinese coolies sometimes when we insist on studying and learning in the *same old way*, not because it is an efficient way, but because it is the way we have been doing it for so long?

Although most of us find that changes are made with difficulty, changes must almost inevitably be made. Some of these changes are necessary because of the physical and psychological growth that is characteristic of us as we pass from early childhood to adulthood.

# WHAT IS NORMAL FOR A CHILD

## MAY NOT BE NORMAL

## FOR A TEEN—AGER

FIGURE 4. Old Ways of Doing Things Must Give Way
to New Ways in Learning as Well as in Eating.

When a child abandons a high chair for an ordinary chair
at the table, his chin is but a little above the table and his

mouth is near his food—hence, the food route from plate to mouth is short. For a child of four this is convenient, necessary, and appropriate. As the child grows, first gradually and later more rapidly, his growth from day to day is never apparent to him nor to those around him. Gradual adjustment is made to the growth process but the same short food route from plate to mouth may be insisted on even after the child has entered adolescence and his body proportions have changed so radically that his back must now be arched like a camel's in order that he preserve the shortest portage from plate to mouth. As one's sitting height increases one must change his posture while eating to one more appropriate to his body proportions. As the food route from plate to mouth lengthens, new skills must be established to prevent food from being spilled when carrying it to the mouth. Because these new skills are seldom easily learned, one does see adolescents who insist on sipping the last spoonfuls of soup from the edge of their plates instead of using a spoon, and who exhibit other equally infantile habits.

It is so easy to continue infantile habits when one does not become aware of them. The author remembers a college student who as a small child must have been taught to put on her winter coat by placing the coat in front of her with the lining exposed forward, inserting her arms into the open sleeves, and then throwing her coat (with arms in the sleeves) over her head and shaking the coat down on her shoulders. Now in college, she was still putting on her coat by windmilling it over her head as she had done when a young child in kindergarten. If you can imagine the spectacle this girl created, you will immediately recognize how humorous she appeared and how highly inappropriate her behavior was for a college girl.

## LEARNING HABITS MUST BE
## CHANGED TOO!

Just as changed eating habits and dressing habits are made necessary by growth, so changed study habits are also demanded. For a youngster just beginning school, to attend for fifteen minutes, or ten, or even for five minutes is long and often very fatiguing. His attention span is short. However, as this child grows older, he can attend for longer and longer periods of time. Whereas formerly he played with a toy for three or four minutes, now he plays with it for twelve or twenty. Early in a child's school career he can attend to reading or writing or arithmetic for only a few minutes at a time because of his characteristically limited attention span. Therefore studying and learning for ten or twelve minutes is appropriate at his age. Suppose, however, that he continues this ten-to-twelve-minute habit after he enters college; then it is as inappropriate and ridiculous as the short food route is for the camel-backed adolescent who insists on keeping his chin an inch from his plate. Not only does the longer attention span of the adolescent make longer study periods possible, but *longer study periods are demanded* because of the complexity of the material learned. Don't expect to continue your primary-grade study habits into college any more than you would continue your primary-grade play interests and reading interests into adulthood.

Suppose you found a person your age still reading:

> I see the ball.
> I see Spot.
> Spot sees the ball.
> I see Spot.
> See. See. See.

What would you think? What do others think of you if your

learning techniques are on the level of a first- or second-grader? The latter is just as absurd as the former, even though it may be somewhat less apparent.

Growth means change—change in all aspects of life. Our methods of learning are no exception. And if we reflect on it but a moment, we realize that we do not want to be infantile in our learning techniques any more than we want to be infantile in our social behavior.

## Why Are We Unwilling to Change?

We noted above that one reason why we are often unwilling to change our learning techniques is because infantile habits are allowed to persist. These early habits are difficult to change because they are the first habits we established, and hence have primacy. Moreover they have been practiced long and therefore are well established. Finally, because we are well acquainted with them, because they are an intimate part of us, we find them comfortable and satisfying—they are easy to follow. We see that there is much in our very make-up that fosters the persistence of these early habits that often resist change so strongly. Yet, changes must be made! Habits must be modified!

Another factor that contributes to this reluctance to accept willingly new attacks on learning is *unconscious resistance to adults*. This is an outgrowth of the psychology of childhood. Adults are bigger than children; they are also stronger, wiser, and better informed. Therefore, they are able to determine the behavior of children, to restrain them from doing this, and to persuade and even to force them to do something else. Perhaps much of this cannot be otherwise; certainly some of it is unavoidable and necessary. Because the child's free activity is interfered with, frustration results and resentment even develops. Thus, an attitude of nonco-

operation, mild in some and stronger in others, is the outcome. This attitude, as so many attitudes, is easily generalized
as an attitude toward all adults, and especially toward those
who exert pressure on the adolescent to make him do those
things which adults think are right and desirable. Since the
*necessity* of studying and learning frequently is emphasized
more than the *interest* aspects of learning, the attitude of
noncoöperation with adults crops out. Therefore, adolescents
may refuse to adopt and establish new modes of effective
learning for no better reason than that *it is something that
adults want them to do.* Continuing the old, inefficient learning habits is a somewhat indirect way of "getting it back" on
one's teachers, parents, and counselors who are so anxious
that you effect a change. It is not so much that you do not
want to learn more with less effort, as it is that you want to
show adults that you are able to direct your own activities.
Really, then, what your resistance reveals is a struggle for
independence, an attempt to achieve status as an adult, and
to prove something to the adults around you, namely, that
you no longer are a child.

Normal as this reaction is, it is unfortunate when one
chooses the area of study behavior as the area in which to
*prove* one's maturity by resistance. Accept the leadership of
interested, willing, and concerned adults who are eager to
assist you to achieve fuller self-realization rather than fight
the battle alone for the sake of self-expression.

A final aspect of this negative psychology toward improving study habits is the emphasis put on the *goal of knowing*
rather than on the *process of learning* which ultimately leads
to achievement of the goal of knowing. Too often we want to
finish the task of learning and thus dispose of it. "Get it over
with and forget it." This is an all too common attitude. When
this is the case, we care little about the method of getting to

FIGURE 5. Is Your Emphasis on the *Goal of Knowing* or on the *Process of Learning* that Enables You to Achieve Your Goal?

our destination for our chief concern is with our arrival. This view engenders the attitude that any method of learning, no matter how bunglesome it may be, is as good as any other method of learning. True, one can climb over a mountain by following a goat trail or even by scaling the face of a cliff, but at what expense to oneself! How much better to follow the highway that was built for the purpose! With learning, it is the same. Any old method *may* get us there, but efficient methods will get us there more quickly and with less expenditure of time and energy.

Now that we have gained insight into the ways in which some people operate and perhaps know some of the reasons for our own resistance to improving our learning habits, let us take several positive steps that will enable us to *learn more with less effort.*

# 2.

## *Learning and Motivation*

### OUR PROBLEM

THE key word in learning, as in any type of achievement, is action. Learning is never passive. One does not just
soak up information and knowledge without effort. Learning
is an active process; it is a process of doing.

Motivating a learner presents a two-fold problem: first,
there is the problem of getting action of any kind, and second,
of directing the action into useful channels that are goal-
oriented.

Getting action is generally called *motivation*. Motivation
is a major problem in learning because of our rather natural
tendency to seek to achieve equilibrium which leads ultimately to complete inactivity. Then, too, there is that factor
of inertia that keeps us from being active. Surely you have
observed what an effort it is to roll out of bed in the morning
even though you know that you have so little time to dress,
eat breakfast, and get to the bus stop. Sometimes it seems you
just cannot get going. Each evening you may be faced with
a similar situation. There is that homework that keeps staring
you in the face, that must be done or you will face failure the
next day. Yet how much easier it is to just sit and procrasti-

nate. "If I could only get started," you moan, yet starting is still postponed. *Motivation is a problem!*

## HOW TO GET ACTION

How can one get another person to act? For that matter, how can one get oneself to act? Your alarm clock has sounded repeatedly and run down completely, you have been called three times, and even though you must be at an eight o'clock class in Scott Hall, several blocks away, in thirteen minutes, you still are in bed. That action is imperative is obvious. How is this action to be obtained? There is, of course, the cold-water treatment. Someone could douse you with a pailful of ice water. This, without a doubt, would induce action but it would not guarantee that you will be in Room 315 Scott Hall in thirteen minutes. Action can be secured, as in this case, by creating a situation that the person will do much to get out of as quickly as possible. True, this is a rather negative approach and you can rest assured that it is very unlikely that anyone will use the above treatment on you, even though you are a very slow morning-riser. Chances are this method will not be avoided because it is a negative approach, but because of the inconvenience it causes and the resulting damage to the mattress.

Give your imagination another fling. Suppose that your wealthy Uncle Jim had the garage man deliver a brand-new sports car to your door as a present to you at the very moment that your roommate called you this morning for the third time. How would you react to his announcement: "Your Uncle Jim has just sent you a new, fire-engine red sports car which is parked outside the front door"? Would you respond with: "Have him drive it around to the garage and remind me to take a look at it after school," and then turn over for another forty winks? You would not! Instead, you would bound out of bed and the house without bedroom slippers and with your housecoat or robe trailing you like Superman's cape! This announcement would certainly get action. Your roommate, no doubt, regrets that he is unable to provide equally effective motivation each school-day morning.

Absurd as both of the above illustrations are (from the standpoint of real life), they do provide a clue to the matter of motivation—the clue which we are seeking. In the cold-water treatment, action is obtained because the sleepy-head has a tendency to avoid the unpleasantness, the coldness, and the wetness which are so in contrast to the comfortable warmth and snugness of his bed. He acts quickly because his pleasantness has come to an abrupt end and a need for action is poignantly present. The sports-car motivator is also effective in obtaining action because the adolescent has such a tendency to be thrilled by large, unexpected presents that he is always ready and eager to accept. It is not that our sleepy-head lacks energy with which to roll out of bed; it is rather that the ringing alarm clock and repeated calls do not arouse in him a tendency to action.

It is now clear that a stimulus is an effective motivator when it arouses a tendency that is a part of the individual's personality. Hence the psychology of motivation is this: *Discover the tendencies that the person has and release them by presenting appropriate stimuli.* This means that to motivate others we must know as much as possible about that which makes them tick. Likewise, if we are to motivate ourselves, as often we must because we cannot wait for others to do that which we must do for ourselves, we must gain insight into the tendencies that we possess and into the ways in which we ourselves can release them most effectively.

To get that action which we call studying, one must dis-

FIGURE 6. Find Ways to Release the Good Tendencies Bottled Up Within You.

cover the tendencies to act that are present in the student and the ways in which those tendencies can be released so that studying results. This is no small task, especially when one tries to discover the available tendencies in oneself and the ways in which they can be released in action. In the following pages, a number of ways in which this can be done and which are known to be effective will be discussed fully.

## DIRECTED ACTION IS NEEDED

Motivation is more than getting action; it is securing *directed* action. In the hypothetical case of the student who overslept and received the cold-water treatment, we can imagine that he acted vigorously after he was made thoroughly uncomfortable, but this is no assurance that his action took a direction that aided him in reaching the classroom by the appointed time. In fact, human nature being what it generally is, he probably reacted with so much emotion that he was fortunate if he arrived at his next class on time.

An assembly-line worker would not hold his job for long if he spent his time actively, even vigorously, tossing nuts and bolts around indiscriminately for eight hours each day. His defense, "Look at all the nuts and bolts I handle each day," would be wholly unacceptable to the efficiency expert whose reply would be, "Yes, but look at what you did with them." Action is not enough. Action must be organized and goal-oriented.

The student who is merely active when he thinks he is studying is no more efficient than the bolt-tossing assembly-line worker. Activity alone does not result in useful work, but organized, directed effort does. This is equally true of the learner. Merely writing words, drawing lines, putting down numbers, or drawing doodles never results in learning; but an organized, systematic, and purposeful approach is very apt to.

More will be said in a later section about the undirected activity that frequently passes for study and the reasons for such activity. See the section in Chapter 4 entitled "Ritual Confused with Learning."

## GOAL-DIRECTED ACTION

Motivation without goals results in blind, random activity. Goals without motivation result in no activity whatsoever, other than daydreaming. Therefore what is accomplished and the value of that which is accomplished depend on the nature of the goals set.

### Grades as Goals

Throughout the school system, from the primary grades through high school, college, and even beyond, emphasis is placed on school grades as a measure of academic success. Promotions are made on the basis of grades; so also are awards, honors, and scholarships given on the basis of grades. Grades determine whether one has the privilege of entering college and the right to remain after entering. Grades *are* important! Because of this great emphasis on grades, it is little wonder that many students make grades their goals.

In the elementary grades emphasis is frequently put on perfection of learning. The child is urged to learn to spell *perfectly,* to make arithmetical computations *without error,* to read with *perfect* diction, to form letters *exactly* like those of the specimen. For high achievement or perfection he is given a "100," an "A," the label "excellent" or something similar. Since nearly every child is urged to achieve to *the* maximum rather than to *his* maximum, a premium is placed on the symbol of achievement rather than on the achievement itself. This attitude is strengthened further by the fact that it is far easier for every child to grasp the importance of the symbol than that which it is supposed to represent. *Hence the grade becomes the goal.*

Among high-school and college students, where the complexity of the academic work is such that achievement is seldom if ever perfect, grades are intended to represent the relative standing of students. Although grades are regarded as objective measures of achievement, they are more often pseudo-objective (falsely objective) in that they are based on a sampling of students' responses (a sampling that may be inadequate) or on teachers' judgments. The true purpose of these grades is to sort students into groups or levels so that the quality of their work can be recorded for future reference and comparison. The true function of grades should be, but seldom is, one of mechanics, of record keeping.

Because our society is a highly competitive society, grades have come to be ends in themselves. The person who gets high grades is honored for his success; the person who gets low ones is condemned for his failure. Because of this commendation and condemnation, some students even resort to dishonesty when high grades cannot be achieved easily or with a moderate amount of effort. When cheating is resorted to as a means of getting a grade, all of one's energy is apt to be concentrated on "beating the game," and learning is lost sight of completely. When this occurs it is deplorable because what are really desired and needed—knowledge and skill—are not obtained even though a grade may be.

Bill was an able student who had done well in all of his courses during his first years in college. Partly because of his academic success and partly because of the scholastic competition offered by a girl friend whom he admired, Bill was determined to graduate from college with high honors. As he approached his last college year, it became increasingly obvious to Bill that a straight-A average in all of his courses was needed, if he were to graduate with high honors. This included a required course in a foreign language, which for Bill meant Spanish. Now, Bill disliked foreign languages because of an earlier difficulty with a language. Realizing that a high grade in the course was unlikely and that his goal of graduating with high honors would not be realized, he went into a slump. When he was present in his Spanish class, which became increasingly unusual, he slept. His daily preparations for his other courses became poorer; he cut classes on the days tests were given, and he overslept frequently. Soon Bill was careless about his appearance and indifferent to the rights and welfare of other people. All this because he failed to make an "A" in Spanish!

Bill, like so many other students, was unable to see that he ran a good race during his college career and that he would have "placed" in the end even though it meant falling short of winning. He failed to see that he had learned much even though honors were not conferred on him. For Bill, the *failure to get a grade meant complete failure* and hence he lost even that which was within his reach.

### Grades as Motivators

There is a great difference between grades as goals and grades as motivators. As we have just seen, when grades become an end in themselves the learner loses sight of that which the grades stand for, his judgment becomes distorted, and in a sense he loses touch with reality. Grades can be motivators when they release in the individual the tendency to learn. When grades serve as motivators they are secondary rather than primary in the individual's thinking; they are that which facilitates the drive to learn. Regarding grades as motives rather than as goals indicates intellectual maturity.

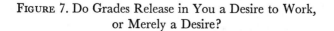

FIGURE 7. Do Grades Release in You a Desire to Work,
or Merely a Desire?

## PROGRESS VERSUS COMPLETION

Why do we learn? A little reflection reveals that we learn facts and skills because they make life easier, more pleasant and interesting, more effective and efficient, and because they enable us to serve others better. Since knowledge and skills are good, it is logical to believe that the sooner we establish them the better. Hence, we concentrate on achievement, which is also desirable. In our eagerness to achieve, however, we too often come to place emphasis on *completion* rather than on *achievement*. In other words, we are more interested in having it done with and over than we are in what we will know or be able to do. We want, somehow, to have our goal behind us rather than before us, and we make completion rather than achievement our goal. Like the emphasis on grades as goals, which we noted before, so overemphasis on completion as a goal is undesirable also. At its worst, this emphasis on completion results in an accumulation of courses taken as though each is another notch in one's gun, or another scalp at one's belt. Courses are taken for their own sake rather than for what one will know or learn. Too often students say, "I had that course," as though it were another gold bar tucked away in their private Fort Knox.

The trouble with the above point of view is that too much emphasis is placed on *knowing* and not enough on *learning*— on the end rather than on the process. This may seem to be a very peculiar thing to say, and you are probably thinking, "The very thing I want is *to know*. There is nothing peculiar about that." You are correct! You are trying to find ways, however, in which we can learn more with less effort, which means that our emphasis is on the process of learning—the process by which we arrive at the stage of knowing.

The all too prevalent notion among students is that the

# THE COURSE ACCUMULATOR

PILES UP CREDITS

# THE STUDENT

USES WHAT HE LEARNS!

FIGURE 8. Which Are You Doing?

important thing is to *complete* the assignment, to write "finis" to the paper. This creates *anxiety* and anxiety actually hinders learning. You know well that when you become anxious to complete an assignment you start cutting corners, and before long you slam the book shut and go in search of more pleasant activities. Emphasis on the completion of a task, or of a course, encourages careless haste and an attitude of finishing one thing and getting on with the next until completion comes to be a veritable compulsion. Needless to say, this attitude is not conducive to learning.

The view stated above can be contrasted with our attitude toward an athletic contest in which one team is definitely in the lead and the winner is hardly in doubt. Even though the outcome of the game is certain, we seldom leave as soon as the winner appears certain. After all, *we did come to see the game* and so we see it through to the finish. We came to see the action, not just to learn the outcome! In the academic situation, as on the contest field or floor, we must emphasize the activity as well as the outcome.

## MOTIVATION BY FORCE

Because our society is more authoritarian than democratic, we have a strong tendency to try to motivate people by force rather than by using the more subtle method of releasing tendencies that was discussed above. This is also true in the educational situation. Here pressures are exerted on students in such ways as to force them to learn, threatening them with failure, humiliation, and even with expulsion when their learning is not satisfactory. Psychological studies of youthful learners working in authoritarian and democratic climates all agree that the democratic climate is far superior to the authoritarian one, in its effect on the learner as well as on his efficiency in learning.

# REACTIONS TO FORCED LEARNING

## Fighting Back

Force generates resistance. When a teacher tries to "make" students learn, he is very apt to find that they resist, sometimes even overtly and with vigor. There are many ways in which students fight back against a teacher. Sometimes it is done by arguing, not logically with the aim of clarifying a point, but with argument for argument's sake. Usually it consists of dogmatic assertions that have a semblance of reason and that are used to confuse and annoy the teacher rather than to arrive at a conclusion. Sometimes this ends in a verbal tug-of-war of yes-no, *yes-no*, YES-NO that is so characteristic of children.

Name-calling, in not too subdued tones so that the teacher may hear, is another way students show their aggression toward an authoritarian teacher. In a few cases, threats of violence are made, and in rare cases actual violence occurs.

Let us examine briefly the psychology of this tendency to fight back. A teacher may command or force a student to do or to attend to something (such as his algebra assignment) when he is doing or attending to something else that he likes to do (such as drawing pictures, daydreaming or annoying a classmate). The teacher's goal for the student is learning; the student's goal is amusement. Because the teacher uses his authority to force the student to do that which he does not want to do, and prevents him from doing that which he is eager to do, the teacher becomes a *barrier* to the free expression of the student's wants and desires. Our rather natural reaction to this type of situation is aggression. We act, sometimes with violence, on the barrier that stands in our way and that prevents the achievement of satisfaction. Hence, the student clashes with the teacher.

Since these student-teacher conflicts occur often, a student may come to react to a certain teacher, or for that matter to any teacher, as a barrier even though he has no clearly defined goal that the teacher is preventing him from achieving at the moment. In this case, the teacher comes to be the sign or the symbol of a barrier to which the student has learned to react with aggression. Formerly this was called redintegration; now it is called conditioning. It is also a case of generalization when the student reacts to almost every teacher with aggression. This generalization is dangerous, for the student who generalizes his aggression will be aggressive even toward those teachers who are not barriers between him and his goals. This generalized hostility actually is a prejudice, and prejudices do not make for good human relations and for sound personal satisfaction.

What can we do about this tendency to fight back? Two ways are open to us. One is to reëvaluate our goals and compare them with those that other people seek to set for us. The other way is to discriminate between those people who are barriers to our future success and happiness and those who merely appear to be. Beware of generalizing! Recognize that most teachers are *not* barriers to your future success and happiness.

## Aggression Toward Others

A second reaction to frustration is aggression toward others. When we are prevented from venting our aggression on the barrier itself, we drain off our frustration by being hostile toward people of whom we are less afraid or those who have little or no authority. The familiar school-ground bully who threatens all his schoolmates and instills fear in most, especially those much younger than he, by his marked aggressiveness is draining off his aggressive feelings by showing hostility toward

FIGURE 9. Reactions to Motivation by Force.

substitutes—perhaps substitutes for his teacher. He dares not hit the teacher (much as he would like to) whom he regards as a barrier, but he does feel free to hit another child who inadvertently gets into his way and who is a less formidable barrier than the teacher.

Aggression toward substitute barriers does not always result in fighting; perhaps more often it gives rise to teasing. Fighting is generally regarded as wrong; teasing is just annoying. The frustrated student would like to hit the teacher, but he knows that this is not sanctioned. Fear that he may not get away with it may also prevent him from hitting another child —but teasing him, that is different. There is no law against teasing, and, besides, the emotion that is exhibited is different. Anger is shown when fighting; pleasantness is exhibited when teasing. Anger is condemned, but not so with pleasantness. Yet, teasing may make the other person angry just as fighting does. Therefore, it may be the teased person who shows the undesirable response (anger) and hence who is condemned. This is just what the teaser wants, and because he has redirected his aggression into a seemingly socially acceptable channel he rids himself of his frustration and tension.

What can we do about this aggression toward others? When hostile feelings plague us because we are frustrated by a teacher or someone else whom we regard as a barrier to our happiness and freedom, we can drain off some or most of the tension by verbalizing. Talk yourself out to a sympathetic listener. In other words, get it off your chest by talking it out. Get the bad feeling out.[1] Usually little harm comes from this, and often much good is derived. It seems to relieve the pressure; it dissipates our emotion of anger. Moreover, it often gives us an opportunity to see the situation and ourselves in a

[1] Dorothy W. Baruch, *New Ways in Discipline,* New York: McGraw-Hill, 1949.

new light. If you have a tendency to tease others excessively and derive a devilish delight from doing it, try to gain insight into the reasons behind your teasing.

Frustration can never be avoided completely. Life just is not like that. We can, however, do something about the way we meet frustration. Are you doing the intelligent thing, or are you channeling your aggression toward others into anger and fighting or teasing?

## Aggression Toward Things

Aggression is not always directed at people; often it is directed at things. Aggression toward people brings strong social condemnation; aggression toward things, especially one's own belongings, is less vigorously disapproved. Who has not seen a student kick his wastebasket or the door, break his pencil, or stamp on his textbook to show his resentment against a professor? Such behavior we refer to as temper tantrums because they are so infantile. Destruction of school property, stealing, and extensive vandalism in school buildings—all are examples of aggression toward things stimulated by frustration.

What can we do about this aggression toward things? We can do what is suggested in the section above, for the psychology of aggression toward things is the same as that of aggression toward people.

## Running Away

Because the above-mentioned ways of reacting to frustration are, for the most part, socially unacceptable, some people run away from a difficult situation. Running away does not hurt the person who was the original barrier, nor does it hurt those around one directly, and it does not result in the destruction of property. Running away from a situation, there-

fore, is a very law-abiding way of meeting frustration. This
does not mean that it is good. When one runs away, he does
nothing that is constructive that will help him meet this or
similar situations in the future. Moreover, when one runs
away from a problem he seeks security, not infrequently in
infantile behavior. Regression to infantile ways of acting is
common because of the feeling of security experienced. The
student who cries, whimpers, or uses baby-talk is acting on
the principle that one just does not punish an infant or require of him that which is required of others. This way of
behaving shows an unwillingness to face reality squarely and
to meet constructively the barriers one inevitably encounters
in life.

What can we do about running away from reality? We
can learn to behave in a mature manner and to accept life
situations as we find them—which also means to accept ourselves. We can learn effective ways of coping with people by
using effective human-relations techniques. Finally, we can
recognize that we never find real security by attempting to
return to the past or by adopting infantile ways.

### Ignoring the Teacher

Some people do not run away from a situation; they merely
ignore it. They behave as though *there is no barrier* between
them and their goal. Whatever they are doing they keep right
on doing, the consequences notwithstanding. A case in point
is the spectator at a fire who, when approaching the burning
building, was warned by a police officer to get away from
there because an explosion was expected at any moment. To
the officer's warning the spectator replied, "There will be no
explosion." This type of person is apt to be a highly self-
centered person, one who shuts out everyone else by building
up a wall around himself that is intended to bolster his own

insecurity. Because he ignores others, he becomes so unrealistic that he often believes that anything he says or does must be right *just because he says and does so.* If he says that there is life on the moon, there *is* life on the moon. If he says that his solution to a chemistry problem or translation of a French passage is correct, *he is correct,* regardless of the professor and the textbook. This type of person is usually rather difficult to deal with because he is out of touch with reality. He lives in, but not as a part of, society.

What can we do about this type of behavior? Often one can do little for this type of person. He does not allow us access to his personality. Therefore, he is among the more baffling types of cases to deal with. Most of us just do not know how to respond to the person who is almost completely unresponsive. Prevention, rather than a cure, is what should concern us. We must learn to live with people, for we cannot live successfully without them.

## Appearing to Coöperate

A final way in which people react to the frustration caused by barriers is by appearing to coöperate with the professor without actually doing so, or by coöperating only partially. This reaction is manifested in a number of ways.

*Use of careless script.* One way in which students appear to coöperate without actually doing so is by writing illegibly and carelessly when writing answers to test questions or when preparing special reports. By their so doing, the teacher is inconvenienced and his job of reading and correcting papers is made more difficult. Sometimes this effort to make the teacher's task difficult is unconscious; at other times it is deliberate. When it is intentional, it shows an attitude of: "Let him figure it out. He is the one who made me do this work anyway." The student who shows his frustration in this way hopes that the teacher will infer that his poor script is due to a lack of skill in handwriting, and that the teacher will never suspect that he is writing poorly intentionally. In any case, he believes that he cannot be accused of deliberately annoying the teacher. He feels safe, yet, secretly, he is trying "to get it back on the teacher."

*Quantity versus quality of work.* A second way of appearing to coöperate without actually doing so is to do great quantities of work, often of inferior quality, so that the teacher must read a great deal of material in order to evaluate the student's work. This too appears to be very defensible, for apparently the student is coöperating very well in that he has put much time and energy into the preparation of his paper. If his motive, however, is to create much work and inconvenience for the teacher, then it is an indication of reaction to frustration. I hasten to point out that every long paper or question fully answered is not an indicator of poor adjustment. Only when the student thinks, "I'll make the teacher work hard and make him sorry that he required so much of us," is his behavior an indicator of frustration due to a barrier.

*Procrastination.* A third way of appearing to coöperate is to procrastinate in completing assignments and presenting required work. In this case, the student frequently reaffirms his good intention to do the required work and to complete the assignment. Therefore, he cannot be accused openly of noncoöperation because his attitudes and intentions appear to be very wholesome. The fact of the matter may be, however, that the student really is thinking: "Let him wait. I'll hand in the material when I get good and ready." The student's psychology is based on an appearance to coöperate while at the same time doing all he can to harass and frustrate the teacher. This he does as a means of giving vent to his own frustration.

The psychology of apparent coöperation is readily determined.  Appearing to coöperate is a more socialized way of
retaliating against a barrier than is fighting back, or than aggression against other people and objects. Moreover, the apparent emotion is one of pleasantness and the apparent
attitude one of coöperation, both of which can hardly be
condemned. For these reasons, this method of showing frustration is much less annoying to the person who is the barrier
than those mentioned earlier.

What can we do about this tendency to sham coöperation?
We can recognize our motives and refuse to hide behind what
appears to be social respectability. Recognition of one's motives is the first step in changing one's behavior. If you are
only an *apparent* coöperator, take that first step of recognizing your motives and then follow it up by becoming a *genuine*
coöperator.

## THE INTEREST MOTIVE

### What Is an Interest?

Of the several ways in which teachers seek to motivate students, the chief one is stimulating interest. The word "interest" is familiar to each of us, but for the sake of clarity, let us
examine it with care and see what this familiar word really
means to us. We say that we are interested in romantic movies, clothes, model airplanes, baseball, swimming, popular or
classical music, scouting, reading, and scores of other things.
What does interest in these things mean?

In the first place, it means that we make a positive or out-
going response toward something. We approach the object
or we participate in the activity—we do not withdraw from it.
Quite literally, we face it rather than turn our back on it. In
the second place, interest implies that pleasure is derived from

FIGURE 10. The Four Phases of Interest.

the object of one's interest. Interest and pleasure tend to go together in degree: the more pleasure derived the greater the interest. Interest, however, is more than sheer pleasure, it is also a symbolic or an intellectual activity. It is something that you *think* about. An idiot does not have interests. Intelligence is an essential ingredient of interest. Therefore, our third point is that an interest is an intellectual activity. Finally, an interest is a pursuit; it is something that one does. We do not say that baseball is our interest if we never play the game or follow the games played by favorite teams. Neither do we claim to have an interest in reading, if we seldom read. Interest implies doing something. Persistent participation generally results in a measure of skill or mastery, and as skill increases, interest grows.

An interest, then, is a positive set or attitude toward something, from which we derive a measure of pleasure, that we think about, and that we pursue actively.

### How Do Interests Develop?

One thing is certain, you can never be interested in something of which you are completely ignorant. Are you interested in a ziggurat or in the Sakai? It is quite likely, never having heard of a ziggurat, that you do not know whether it is an old type of musical instrument, an ancient Babylonian tower, or a favorite type of food in Germany. As for Sakai, you may be thinking that it is a new comic-strip character with whom you are as yet unacquainted. The fact is that a ziggurat is an ancient Babylonian temple tower built like a pyramid, and the Sakai are a Malayan tribe of people. Should you read extensively and become better informed on the beauty of a ziggurat tower, and the characteristics of the Sakai people, it is possible for you to develop an intense interest in either or both of these subjects.

*Primacy of knowledge.*   You may have a mild interest in
physiotherapy, accountancy, or designing as a future occupation. Your interest is weak and uncertain because you have
some knowledge, but not a great deal, of what a physiothera-
pist, accountant, or a designer really does. On the other hand,
you may have an intense interest in photography because
you know a great deal about the composition of pictures,
color developing, and printing, and the principles of chemistry and physics that are involved. Interest generally increases with knowledge, but *there can be no interest unless
there is some knowledge first.* Knowing stimulates the growth
of interest.

*Derived pleasure.*   We pointed out above that we are interested in those activities which give us pleasure. You may
be interested intensely in dogs and hence willing to pet and
befriend every dog you see, and especially those that look
bedraggled or mistreated. "I just love dogs," you say, when
someone chides you for being so concerned about each stray
dog you see. If this is the way you feel about dogs, it is quite
possible that, when you were quite young, you were given a
puppy with whom you grew up. He followed you everywhere
you went; he slept at the foot of your bed each night; he
licked your face when you cried. Your dog was your best
friend, and became associated with pleasant experiences. Now
the very sight of a dog suggests pleasure. Psychologists call
this conditioning. We can come to respond with pleasure, or
with annoyance, to almost anything; but whether it will be
pleasure or annoyance will depend on the nature of our experiences.

*Skill and mastery.*   Interest in painting, in sewing, in elec-
tronics, in sports, or in anything else, develops as skill and
mastery develop. Recall your first experiences with tennis or
golf or some other activity that has become a hobby. Your

# DO THIS

# AVOID THIS

POSITIVE ATTITUDE

NEGATIVE ATTITUDE

*I KNOW I'LL LIKE MATH*

POSITIVE VERBALIZATION

*I KNOW I'LL HATE MATH*

NEGATIVE VERBALIZATION

ADEQUATE KNOWLEDGE

INADEQUATE KNOWLEDGE

SATISFACTION

ANNOYANCE AND
FRUSTRATION

FIGURE 11. Do's and Don't's for Developing Interest in School Subjects.

interest was intensified after you could win a game, come close to par, or even make a hole in one! Interest increases not only with knowledge but with skill as well.

*Importance of aptitude.* Skill depends in part on aptitude. Even given the same opportunity and the same instruction, each of us does not develop the same degree of skill, and, hence, not the same interests. This is due somewhat to the differences in our aptitudes. Many of us just do not have what it takes to become a racing-car driver or a skilled musician. For this reason, we may have little or no interest in these activities. It is doubtful that one can become interested in just anything or in everything that interests other people.

## Interest in School Subjects

Now that we have examined the psychology of interest with considerable care, let us apply what we know to the learning of school subjects. How can we acquire an interest in school work and in school subjects?

*The positive attitude.* The very first point that we made concerning interest was that *it is a positive attitude.* This means that we must be willing to learn. Willingness is the very first essential. When we approach a school subject in the spirit, "I dare the teacher to make me interested," the chances are great we will not become interested. When we dare someone, we show a stubborn unwillingness to change. We serve notice that we are not open to conviction. We are defiant—we are convinced that we are right. Needless to say, interest does not grow in this kind of soil.

Interest has a chance to grow when one takes the attitude, "I shall give it a fair trial. I do not know now whether or not I shall be interested in this school subject that I am taking, but I shall not make a decision concerning it until I know more about it. Who knows, I may become very much interested in it and I do not want to lose this opportunity until I am quite certain that I know what I am doing." This attitude, in contrast to the I-dare-you attitude, gives interest in that particular subject an opportunity to grow. The reason some students do not give themselves the opportunity to discover the presence of an interest in a particular school subject is that they are afraid that *they may become interested.* If this is the reason, why are they afraid?

*The importance of verbalization.* Often students say: "I just know I will hate biology, or Latin, or mathematics, or English, or history!" This expression of attitude prior to taking a subject is unfortunate. I recall, during my own early adolescence, that I once said, "I do not like sauerkraut" when it was passed to me at dinner one day. I do not know what possessed me to say that I did not like sauerkraut, because it was not true. However, having once said, "I do not like sauerkraut," I did not feel that I could go back on what I had said, eat sauerkraut, and remain consistent. The result was that I did not eat sauerkraut for a considerable time after that.

Positive statements of attitude not only keep us from eating sauerkraut; they also keep us from developing interests in science or history or languages as well. The student who has told his friends, not once but many times, that he *knows* that he will dislike Government or French finds it difficult, after several weeks of the course, to admit to his friends that he really finds the work interesting and even stimulating. He has committed himself in the past and he cannot bear to think how his friends will react to his unexpected change in attitude. So what does he do? He goes right on saying that he hates Government or French and at the same time tries hard to convince himself that what he is saying is true. The danger is that what he says may win out over his deeper inclination. Don't let this happen to you!

*The importance of knowledge.* Are you interested in astronomy? Of course, you may *say* that you are or that you are not interested, but you do not really *know* until you have some knowledge of this science. If you have visited an observatory and peered through a large telescope at the rings of Saturn or the moons of Jupiter, and have had the good fortune to be able to attend one or several lectures at one of the planetariums, then you do know something about astronomy. Limited though your knowledge may be, yet it is a basis for interest. As your knowledge is increased by repeated visits to observatories, and by the reading of popular or authoritative books on the subject, your interest in astronomy is given an opportunity to grow. Naturally, this is no assurance that your interest will increase; in fact, it may decrease after you encounter the mathematical aspects of astronomy. But *without knowledge it simply cannot grow.*

This is equally true of all the school subjects that you are studying. As you extend your reading vocabulary, the fine distinctions and the niceties of expression in poetry and in prose come to interest you. As you learn new idioms and more complex verb forms in German that enable you to express your thoughts to others more adequately, your interest in German is likely to increase. As you gain insight into simple and more complex electrical circuits, your interest in the mechanics of radio and television increases. Even as you learn the more technical terms and rules of a sport, the more enthusiastic you become about that sport.

Since this necessary knowledge of school subjects often comes slowly and with much effort, one must have patience. Interest does not necessarily blossom on first contact with a subject. Interest, we have said, is a growth process, not an inoculation, and *growth always takes time.* Therefore, always allow yourself enough time to gain a reasonable acquaintance with a subject. Give interest a chance to grow!

*The conditioning process.* The linking of pleasantness or unpleasantness with various objects and activities, we called conditioning in an earlier section. This process occurs whether we are aware of it or not. If each time you made a mistake when typing, you received a mild electric shock in the fingers from the typewriter, you would soon learn (be conditioned) to withdraw your fingers quickly from the keyboard as soon as an error would be made. The pain in your fingers would become tied up with errors in such a way that you would respond to the sight of an error as you did formerly to the shock in the fingers, even though no shock is now given. Now you would be withdrawing due to the *sight of an error,* a thing you did not do in the beginning.

Let us see how conditioning operates in the ordinary school situation. Let us suppose that because you did not do well in your algebra course last semester, you absented yourself from the class as often as possible so as to get away from the unpleasant subject and the teacher who taught it. This semester you are taking history from the same teacher and already you are cutting class as often as you can, even though formerly you were interested in history. You have become conditioned to respond to this teacher by withdrawing, and so you are now withdrawing from the teacher and the subject even though there is no valid reason (other than conditioning) for doing so.

Conditioning works positively as well as negatively. When pleasant experiences become linked with a school subject, interest rather than withdrawal results. Associate as many pleasant experiences with each school subject and the teacher as possible until finally any mention of that subject invariably arouses pleasantness.

*Using conditioning.*   How can pleasantness be associated with a particular school subject? Various things can be done. A correct response in class will make you feel that you have made a contribution to the class, that you are a part of the class, and the feeling is pleasant. An intelligent question, one that shows insight, asked during a class discussion has the same effect on a person. A completed, rather than a half-completed, assignment results in pleasantness and relaxation because one knows that he is prepared. Extra work beyond that which has been assigned as the minimum pays dividends in interest. Promptness in completing assignments and neatness in one's work are among the little things that create pleasantness. When one experiences pleasantness frequently or even daily from the doing of these and similar things in a particular course, gradually the course itself comes to stand for pleasantness. Now you are conditioned to respond positively to that school subject. And *positive response is essential to interest.*

*The need for skill.*   In an earlier section we pointed out that interest grows with the achievement of skill. As an example, recall your early efforts at learning to play the piano, the trumpet, or the violin. Do you remember all those wrong keys you struck and the sour notes you produced during the first weeks and months, due to your lack of skill? During those early months, did you practice because of an intense interest in mastering the instrument or because of someone's insistence? More than likely, it was the latter. As you developed skill and a measure of mastery, however, you were prodded less, not because of the prodder's weariness, but because you were now practicing voluntarily due to your own interest in music. If you failed, you probably stopped taking lessons entirely because your parents finally conceded that you had little or no interest in music.

When learning academic things, skill makes for interest also. In fact, in the development of interest, skill goes beyond knowledge. Knowing certain facts and principles in a school subject, as we stressed above, makes for interest; but *skill in the use of* these facts and principles makes for even greater interest. Don't be satisfied with *just knowing* conjugations and declensions in the foreign language you are studying; achieve *skill* in conjugating and declining so that you can put some *speed* into the doing of it. Don't be satisfied with just knowing how to add a column of figures; but learn number combinations so that you can add skillfully with speed and accuracy. *Supplement knowledge with skill* and even you will be surprised at the intensity of your interest. Remember that you like, that you are interested in, that which you do well.

Is interest in every school subject possible? This question cannot be answered with an unequivocal "Yes" or "No." For most of us, some interest can be developed in many, if not most, of the school subjects taken. In fact, it is quite likely that, being the normal person that you are, you can develop a measure of interest in all of the school subjects you are now taking. Hence, the answer to the above question may be "Yes."

On the other hand, your attention was called earlier to the fact that aptitude is a factor in interest. A tone-deaf person can hear, but he cannot hear pitch differences. Lacking aptitude in the perception of pitch differences, he will not develop an interest in music. Neither will a color-blind person develop an interest in visual art that features color.

The student who lacks reading aptitude due to an eye defect or ocular incoördination generally lacks interest in reading. Some people seem to lack verbal aptitude. We find that interest in foreign languages, grammar, and writing is generally low in these people. Still other people lack mechanical aptitude, or artistic aptitude, or scientific aptitude and, therefore, they are not interested in things mechanical, artistic, or scientific. From this point of view the answer to our question is "No."

Don't take too much comfort in this negative answer. Although it is true that some aptitude is necessary for interest development, you had better be certain that you lack aptitude before you use that as an excuse for your lack of interest in particular school subjects. Lack of interest is much more likely to be the result of a lack of application, a lack of knowledge and of skill, than of a lack of aptitude. Since many aptitudes can be measured adequately with standardized tests, check your aptitude. Do not just guess at it, for when you guess, your judgment is biased by your desire. Measure your aptitude. You may be surprised at how much aptitude of a given sort you really have. Use your aptitude as a basis for interest development!

# 3.

# *What Is Learning?*

## LIVE AND LEARN

### Learning Is Characteristic of All Life

Inky, your pet dog, has learned many interesting things, thanks to your patience and training. One of the earliest things he learned was to sit up and "speak" for food. Before long, frisky Inky also learned to lie still when you said, "Play dead dog"; he learned to follow close behind you in response to the command "Heel," when being walked, and to return home when you commanded him in a stern voice, "Go home, Inky." Eventually Inky even learned to stop chasing the neighbor's cat and to stay out of their flower bed. Inky, you must admit, has learned a great deal.

Dogs are not the only pets that learn. You may know of a parakeet that has a sizeable vocabulary, a cat that jumps through a hoop or walks on its hind legs, or a pet skunk that knows ever so many tricks.

Circus animals also give us many illustrations of animal learning. There are the performing seals that balance large balls on their noses, bears that roller-skate and ride bicycles, horses that dance remarkably well, and elephants that learn

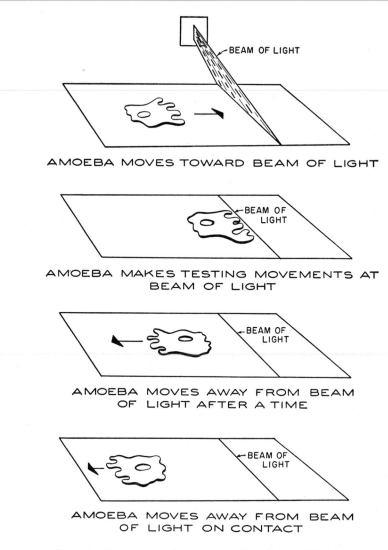

FIGURE 12. Amoebas Learned to Recoil from Light and
to Move Away in the Opposite Direction in 6 to 27
Trials. Adapted from S. O. Mast and L. C. Pusch,
"Modification of Response in Amoeba," *Biol. Bull.*,
1924, *46*: 55–59.

so many interesting things, to say nothing of the lions, tigers, chimpanzees, and monkeys.

If you have ever lived on a farm, you know that ordinary barnyard animals learn too. The pigs and the chickens learn to come running when they are called. Ponies sometimes learn to open gates, and even the cows learn to come home each evening at the same time.

In the psychology laboratory many animals have been used in learning experiments, and all of them learn something. Monkeys learn to put two or three jointed sticks together and thus fabricate a tool that they use to rake into their cages food that is out of reach. Chimpanzees have learned even to work for poker chips that they could use in a special device called a "chimp-o-mat." A blue chip in a certain chimp-o-mat "bought" a grape, a red chip in another chimp-o-mat gave a piece of apple, and a white one in still another "bought" water. White rats learn quickly to find their way through a complicated maze and then remember the correct path for a considerable time, once it has been thoroughly learned.

That these animals learn may not seem strange to you because all are higher animals with fairly well-developed nervous systems. What about lower animals? Do they learn too? Yes, they do. Not only do turtles and oysters learn, but such aquatic life as stentor, the sea anemone, and such microscopic life as the paramecium and the one-celled amoeba learn. There is even some evidence that some plants may learn, as was true in the case of some marigolds that modified the opening and closing of their blossoms (sleep movement).[1]

Although we cannot prove that every form of life, including plants, learns, we can safely say that *all forms of animal life have the potentiality to learn.*

[1] C. J. Warden, T. N. Jenkins, and L. H. Warner, *Comparative Psychology,* II, New York, Ronald Press, 1940, 286.

INFANTS LEARN

CHILDREN LEARN

ADULTS LEARN

OLD PEOPLE
LEARN

FIGURE 13. Learning Is Characteristic of All Ages.

## One Never Stops Learning

All too many people associate learning just with one's childhood and youth, as though it were something that one does only when in school. It is true that learning is given considerable emphasis during one's early life and school years; in fact, learning in our society is the child's chief business. This does not mean, however, that when one graduates from high school or even from college, one stops learning. Certainly, the learning that one does after graduation may be less formal than before, but it is learning nevertheless.

Every time you take a new job, you must acquire new knowledge and learn new skills. Even when you continue with the same job, new things must be learned. The automobile mechanic must learn new ways of repairing cars each time a new model appears on the market, and that is *each year*. Every innovation in a dictograph, bookkeeping machine, or other business machine requires the office secretary to learn something new. Many adults who have driven cars with standard gear shifts for years have had to learn to drive cars with automatic gear shifts in recent years. No matter how long one lives, as long as he participates in the activities going on around him, *there is need for learning*. Fortunately, we can meet this need. We can continue to learn even when we rival the patriarch Methuselah in longevity!

Because learning is a life-long proposition, not just a childhood activity, let us establish early such learning techniques that throughout life we shall be able to continue *to learn more with less effort*.

## The Need for Learning

Learning seldom occurs unless there is a need for learning. By need we mean that it is desirable or necessary to learn certain things—that there is some compulsion that motivates the learning. On occasion, some of our learning is incidental (not needed, not motivated) learning. You may remember, for no good reason, the five grocery items you purchased on the twenty-third of last month, or the exact date of the last school fire drill. Since no effort was made to learn these items, they are examples of incidental learning. Incidental learning is learning that occurs with little or no effort and which has little or no relationship to other things learned. Incidental learning is unintentional learning. Learning that is accomplished because of a need, requires some effort (sometimes a great deal of effort), generally is intentional, and is more likely to be related to other things learned.

That there is a need, however, does not guarantee that learning results. Look at your handwriting critically. Is it easy to read? Can a person unfamiliar with your handwriting read it easily? Can you read your last week's notes with ease? Unless you are exceptional in this skill, your handwriting most likely is difficult to read and at times even is illegible. The *need for improvement* is there, but this is no assurance that improvement will result. In fact, it is more than likely that your script is poorer today than it was a couple of years ago. Not until you recognize that there is a need for improvement in your handwriting will there be any. That day when you say to yourself, "I must improve my handwriting, because even I can't read it," you will make a beginning in learning to write more legibly. That day the need for improvement will be recognized—it will become a felt need. The recognition of the need for learning, this intention to learn, is essential for the type of learning we are concerned with in this book.

If we hope to learn more with less effort, *we must begin with the intention to learn.* Our learning must be *purposeful, goal-oriented, and motivated by candid recognition of the presence of a need for learning.* This does not imply that it will be effortless, as incidental learning is. Worth-while learning always means work! Recognizing the presence of the need for learning, let us strive to learn how to learn in the most effective and efficient way.

## THE DEFINITION OF LEARNING

### Modification of Behavior

The word "learning" is another of those familiar words that we use again and again but seldom pause to analyze. What really does "learning" mean? When we learn we do two things: (1) we do something in a way which is different from the way we have done it before, and (2) we continue to do it in this new way for some time. In other words, we *effect a modification* in our behavior and we *retain* this modified behavior for some time. There is one additional point that is essential to our concept of learning, namely, this modification of behavior must be due to *experience* rather than disease or degeneration. Learning, then, is the *retention* of behavior that has been *modified* through *experience.*

That learning implies the retention of a modified response does not mean that the changed response must be retained permanently or even for a long period of time. You may learn now that Jehu is the name of the reckless chariot-eer mentioned in the Bible,[2] and should someone ask you to name this reckless charioteer after you have completed reading this chapter you probably will still reply that Jehu is the man. But suppose someone asks you a month or even ten days from now to name the Biblical character who was the reckless charioteer, will you say that it is Jehu or will you say, "It is Joshua or Jehoshaphat or something like that"? The fact that perhaps you will not recall the man's

[2] II Kings, 9:20.

name even tomorrow does not mean that no learning occurred. Something was learned and retained, but not for long. Sometimes, of course, we effect modifications in our behavior that we retain as long as we live. One day during your spelling period your teacher taught you the correct spelling of the word "lieutenant" by pointing out that all you need to remember is the somewhat meaningless phrase, "lie you ten ant." Since that day you have not forgotten that "lieutenant" is spelled *lie-u-ten-ant*.

Learning, we are saying, occurs any time we do something in a way that differs from the way we have been doing it because of experience, and retain or remember that new way for a short or for a long time.

### Learning and Improvement

Generally, when we think of learning we think of it in terms of improvement; we think of others or ourselves as doing something *better* than the way it was done before. Although improvement is generally implied in much of the learning that we are concerned about, it is not characteristic of all learning. A moment ago we called attention to your handwriting and the fact that it may be less legible now than at some time in the past. This deterioration in your handwriting is a case of *learning to write more poorly!* Your present careless script is certainly a modification from what it was formerly, and since you are persisting in writing this way, it certainly is learned.

Youngsters brought up in homes where correct English is spoken learn to use "he don't," "ain't," and "it's me" from some of their schoolmates even though they used correct English prior to entering school. This too is learning, but it is not learning in the direction of improvement.

In order that learning result in improvement it must be

goal-oriented; it must be directional. Although any behavior modification that is retained is learning, improvement results when those modifications approach or approximate a certain standard of behavior that is generally set by the society in which we live. Let us remember that merely changing our behavior and fixing those changes is not enough; we must always be aware of the direction of those changes.

## TRIAL-AND-ERROR LEARNING

### A Primitive Type of Learning

Father has just driven into the driveway with a brand-new car. You bound out of the house and request, with some insistence, permission to drive the new car. Knowing that you are a careful driver, your father obligingly gives you the key along with a few admonitions concerning safe driving. Eager to get going, you try to insert the key, notches up, into the lock; failing in this, you insert the key smooth side up into the lock and start the car. Later, still eager to drive the new car and show it off to friends, you are so intent on "going places" that you pay no attention to the way the key must be inserted into the lock. By sheer chance you insert it correctly about fifty per cent of the time, and since the delay in making a wrong response is so slight, you pay no attention to the proper way of inserting the key. After many *trials* you may come to insert it smooth side up each time without knowing that that is what you do. In fact, should someone ask you which way the key must be inserted into the lock— notched side or smooth side up—you would in all probability not be able to tell him.

This type of learning generally is called *trial-and-error* learning. Sometimes it has been called trial-with-accidental-success learning. That is just what it was in your case—trial and accidental success. This type of learning is a blind type

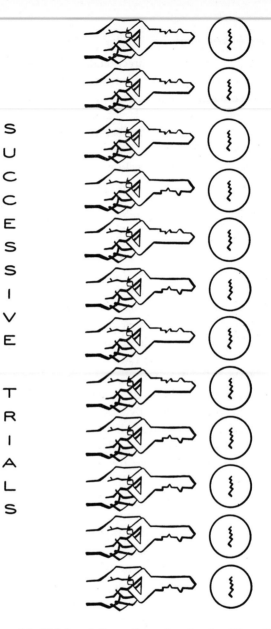

FIGURE 14. Trial-and-Error Learning in the Use of a Car Key.

of learning. It is blind either because one cannot foresee which response will be the correct response, or because one is unwilling to examine the situation with sufficient care to discover which is or is likely to be the correct response.

## Factors Involved

*Persistence in selection.* We pointed out above that learning involves the modification and fixation of response, but there is another point that we must also stress, namely, the need for *persistence in selection,* from one's repertory of responses, of the adequate or the correct response.

Let us suppose that someone gave you a key ring with 25 keys, all very much alike in appearance and only one of which unlocked a given door, and asked you to learn which key it is. You could, of course, attack the problem systematically by taking the first key to the right of the bunch, try it, then try the second key from the right, and so on until you found the right key. If you are more typical in your approach, you will try a key at random; failing, you will try another key at random, and so on until the door is unlocked. Either approach to the problem is trial and error in nature, but the second is typically so. In this type of situation there is no way in which you can *foresee* which key (which response) is going to be the correct one. Therefore, the choice of the right one, whether it comes early or late in the series of responses, is purely accidental. If the learner gives up without success after trying the eighth, or the sixteenth, or even the twenty-fourth key, he will fail to unlock the lock. *He must persist in trying until he finds the right key.*

Some of the day-to-day situations that we must learn to meet we can meet only by the use of trial-and-error learning. Some people fail in this type of learning because they do not persist in trying out new methods of attack on the problem until an adequate solution is found. Since it is a chance affair, it may be the last "try" as well as the first that gives success. In the illustration of the 25 keys, it may be the twenty-fifth, or the first, or any other key that unlocks the lock. The trouble with some learners is that they think they must always be successful in the first two or three attempts. They fail to continue to sample the many other alternatives open to them.

Persistence is essential to success in trial-and-error learning. If one does not continue to search for the correct response until it is discovered, and then continue to rediscover it until it is fixated, no adequate learning is possible.

*Conscious fixation.* Having discovered the right key from among the 25 possibilities, one could lose contact with it after unlocking the lock and let it drop back into the bunch of keys with no way of identifying it later. If this were done, the whole laborious process of selection would have to be repeated. This might be done many times with little or no learning as to which key is the right one. Eventually, of course, one might discover certain cues that would help in earlier identification of the key that is wanted. In any case, this would be a very slow way to learn to meet a situation.

Although little can be done to speed up the initial process of selection in trial-and-error learning, much can often be done as to the fixation of the correct response. Continuing with our illustration of the 25 keys, let us suppose that having found the right key we now *consciously identify* it in some way. This may be done by noting that when we hold the ring of keys before us with the notched sides facing us and with the identification tag to the right of the keys, the correct key is the seventh from the right. Having identified the key in this way, we can always find it on a moment's notice. When you consciously fixate a correct response, you *relate* it in one or more ways to other things you already know.

Learning that is limited to the trial-and-error approach is almost invariably slow; when it is supplemented by *conscious fixation of the correct response,* it is speeded up considerably. Therefore, *persist* until you find the correct response to the problem situation you must meet, and after you have found that correct response, *fixate it consciously* so that the next time you meet this same situation you will be able to identify the correct response more easily and more quickly.

## The Lazy Learner

Trial-and-error learning is often used by the lazy learner because he prefers acting to thinking. It seems easier to move a muscle than to manipulate symbols in thought. Take the case of a student trying to solve a mathematical problem that he knows little about. Not knowing how to proceed, he may first try adding the numbers, but failing to get the answer he knows to be correct, he attempts dividing the first number into the second, then the second into the first, all without any apparent insight or success. This he may do over and over again even though he knows that in all previous attempts he failed to find the desired answer. Should this inept student of mathematics finally perform the correct mathematical process that would give him the desired answer, he probably would be satisfied and do nothing to discover why his procedure gave him the desired result. In other words, this student would do nothing to fixate his correct response and, hence, his next attempt to solve a similar (or even the same) problem would be done in the same bungling way as before.

If one hopes to learn more with less effort, one must *consciously fixate correct responses* when they are discovered. This is the only way in which one can make steady progress toward improvement and ultimate mastery of day-to-day problems. This fixation, as we stated earlier, is accomplished by *knowingly attending* to the significant relationships between the correct response and other things that one observes and knows. This is what we did in our illustration of the 25 keys.

## LEARNING AS REPRODUCTION

### Rote Learning

Too often, students think of learning, and particularly ideational learning, as nothing more than reproduction. In fact, there are those students who prefer to learn by rote. By rote learning we mean the *verbatim reproduction of ideational material.* Just as in trial-and-error learning we found that the learner who has an aversion for thinking falls back on motor manipulation in preference to reasoning, so the ideational learner may prefer rote learning to more discriminating methods. Rote learning is easier; one does not have to think much. One just reproduces the words mechanically. Students often memorize poetry or prose with emphasis on *reproduction* rather than on *meaning—completion* rather than *comprehension.* Is it any wonder that at a later time they scarcely remember having reproduced the material earlier?

Rote learning has often been advocated as a means of learning factual material. One such illustration is the jingle: "Thirty days hath September, April, June, and November; all the rest have thirty-one, save February alone, which has twenty-eight, except once in four when leap year makes it twenty-nine." True, one can learn the number of days in each month by this method, but it is a bit cumbersome when one has to stop to think: "Is July among those months that have but thirty days?" Then realizing that it is not among them, one concludes that it must have thirty-one days. This is a round-about way of learning something that can be learned directly more easily. Would it not be simpler to learn with *conscious attention* the four months, April, June, September, and November, that have but thirty days each?

The danger of rote learning is that as the material learned becomes better established and can be reproduced with greater and greater ease, there is a tendency to pay less and less conscious attention to what is being reproduced until finally it degenerates into a motor response with which little meaning is associated. It is quite likely that as a child you memorized the Lord's Prayer by rote. Since that time you have, in all probability, repeated it hundreds, perhaps even several thousands, of times; in fact, you have repeated it so many times that now you generally repeat it in a purely automatic way. Because its repetition has become automatic with you, you are now scarcely able to follow its meaning consciously and repeat it at the same time. The very thing that your parents hoped you would be able to do, you now find difficult or nearly impossible to do because you learned the prayer by rote.

Although rote learning has some value at times, do not allow it to replace the more conscious and meaningful learning that is so essential for success in school subjects.

### Memorization

*Is memorization bad?* Don't memorize! Don't memorize! This command has been dinned into your ears by teachers for so long that you not only accept the injunction, you actually avoid memorizing as though it were a vicious virus that no antibiotic will touch. Is memorizing really bad? What do your teachers mean when they admonish you not to memorize? In all probability they have in mind the undesirable aspects

FIGURE 15. When You Memorize, Do You Just Vocalize Like a Parrot, or Do You Preserve Meanings?

of rote learning that we discussed above. When things are memorized by rote, emphasis is entirely on *reproduction* and not at all on *meaning*. Hence, if the rhythm of what is being memorized is preserved in reproducing it, changes may be made in what is said without one's ever knowing that a change has been made. After a few more repetitions, more changes may be made until finally the original meaning is largely lost and all that is left is a ritual—a rather meaningless ritual.

A schoolboy once memorized the pledge of allegiance to the flag as follows: "I pledge a legion to the flag and the Republic of Richard Sands; one nation and a vegetable with liberty and justice for all." [3] Certainly this youngster did not know that he was saying anything different from that which other children were saying; it sounded the same to him. Had this boy ever stopped to think about what he was saying, his own words would have perplexed him. "Isn't schoolwork crazy?" "Why do we have to learn such junk?" More than one child has asked these questions, and for the same reason.

Of course, memorized material that is distorted and meaningless appears "crazy." Because teachers are intent on having you learn *meanings,* which are seldom learned when the method of rote learning is used, they insist: *don't memorize!*

*One must memorize.* Generally, we say that we *memorize* rather than *learn* a poem. We use the word "memorize" in this connection because it implies *exact reproduction.* When learning poetry or prose selections, exactness in reproduction is essential. It is no less important when learning formulas in chemistry and physics, the bones of the body in anatomy, classifications in botany and zoölogy, and declensions and conjugations in foreign languages. With this you may agree readily. "But," you say, "I certainly must *not* memorize his-

[3] A. T. Jersild, *Child Psychology,* 4th ed., New York: Prentice Hall, 1954, p. 458.

tory, or economics, or psychology, or sociology!" No, you must not memorize these subjects, if by memorizing you mean learning line after line of the text until you can repeat literally whole pages of what is printed in a particular textbook. This parrot-like reproduction of the material in a textbook is not the type of learning you want. Your objective is not to be able to repeat to your grandchildren, fifty years hence, the content of a particular text. They will want to read modern textbooks for themselves when that time comes. Your goal in learning is *to know now* the facts, the observations, and the conclusions that you find in the textbook you are studying. Your purpose is not to store up these things for the indefinite future. The purpose of reading and studying *this* book is that *you will learn to know, and how to use, now* those techniques that will enable you to learn more with less effort. Your purpose in reading this book is a practical and immediate one; your purpose in studying other school subjects should be a practical and immediate one also.

The emphasis in all learning should at all times be put on *intelligent comprehension* of what is being learned. Stress *knowing* rather than mere reproduction. Don't become a "talking book"! Be informed, intelligent, and equipped to meet problems as they arise. This is the purpose of learning!

The teacher's command, "Don't memorize," seems to be correct; our goal is not reproduction. But does this mean that *all* memorizing is bad and that there is never a time when we should memorize? Let us examine several illustrations.

In psychology there is a law known as the Weber-Fechner Law. The statement of this law is: Equal relative differences are equally perceptible. This statement is concise and meaningful; it is doubtful that there is any better way of stating it. Therefore, to know the Weber-Fechner Law and to communicate its meaning to someone else, *one must memorize* (learn) the statement: Equal relative differences are equally perceptible.

In every school subject we encounter many terms, some of which are familiar and others new to us, that are defined in particular ways. The word "intelligence" is one such term which may be defined as follows: "Intelligence may be regarded as the ability a person has to use his past experiences in such ways as to meet new situations quickly and effectively." [4] Here is one of many statements of definition of this term. Is there value in memorizing this definition? Yes! For as we analyze it we find that this definition stresses a number of things, namely, that intelligence is *an ability;* that it is an ability to *utilize and employ* (what) one's *past experiences* (how) in such ways as to bring them to bear on *new situations* (not ones you have met hundreds of times before), and that these new situations are met with *speed* and *effectiveness.* To be sure to include all these essential points, one is wise to *memorize* this statement of the definition.

Compare this definition of intelligence with such as one hears frequently given in a class in general psychology: "It's something that you inherit." "It shows how smart you are." "It's something that you need to pass this course." "It's something that makes you feeble-minded when you haven't it." Would it not be better to memorize the definition quoted above (or a similar one) than to use the inadequate statements just cited?

Here is another definition that you can analyze for yourself: "A test is a typical situation, or a group of such situations, that is representative of a more general area of knowledge, skill or behavior, and that affords some numerical or quantitative evaluation of a person's performance in the

[4] G. J. Dudycha, *Psychology for Law Enforcement Officers,* Springfield, Illinois, Charles C. Thomas, 1955, p. 30.

larger area of activity." [5] Compare this definition with such inadequate definitions as these: "A test is something that you have to pass." "A test is a bunch of questions that try to trip you up." "When you have to find answers to problems you have never seen before, that's a test."

To make progress in academic subjects one must possess verbal skills. One must have an adequate vocabulary, know definitions, idiomatic expressions, and symbols. Words are the tools used in working out solutions to new problems—the tools for acquiring new knowledge. Skill in the use of these tools is essential, and skill in these matters is achieved by *memorizing* words, definitions, and the like. Yes, there is a place for memorizing. In fact, there is an indispensable need for it! Memorize! *Memorize those elements of knowledge that will enable you to comprehend more.*

## LEARNING AS DISCOVERY
### Seeing New Relationships

The heart of academic learning is discovering new relationships. In the preceding pages we have stressed repeatedly the need for conscious, intentional learning in which one is keenly aware of the relationships involved in what is dealt with. *Learning,* from one point of view, *is the process of discovering relationships.* When we are poignantly aware of a relationship just discovered, the fact of discovery is generally pleasant, and pleasantness tends to fixate in our minds this new relationship in such a way that we are much less likely to forget it. In fact, some of these discoveries we never forget. Let us see how this process of discovery really works.

Look carefully at Figure 16. What do you see? Without a doubt, you immediately recognize the two symbols as familiar

[5] *Ibid.,* p. 17.

trademarks and you think: G-E, General Electric, large corporation, light bulbs, electrical appliances, or something similar. It is quite likely that you are a bit puzzled by the word "or" separating the two symbols. What does it have to do with the trademarks? Since we are thinking about discovering relationships, you are, no doubt, wondering what else can be perceived in this essentially familiar figure other than "General Electric or General Electric." Perhaps you have repeated the letters "G-E," then the word "or" and the letters

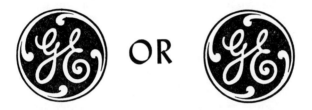

FIGURE 16. What Do You See? (Reproduced with permission of the General Electric Company.)

"G-E" several times. Now you are saying it faster: "G-E or G-E," followed by "G-E o-r G-E," followed by "G-e-o-r-g-e." Then something clicked and you have it—George!

"By George!" you say, "I certainly never before thought of George as two General Electrics connected by the word 'or'!" No, you probably did not, but now that you have, will you ever forget it? I doubt that you will. The name George has taken on a new meaning for you. You made an unexpected discovery and the discovery was a pleasant one. *You have learned a new relationship.*

Much of our learning can be of this type—the type in which we exclaim: "Well, what do you know! I see something new!" When you study, pose questions and seek to discover their answers. Have the type of experience that you had with "G-E or G-E" again and again and find that learning can be fun when you make it *a process of discovering new relationships.*

## Conceptual Learning

A concept is a word or a name that stands for a class of objects or for the relationships or properties that the separate objects have in common. Take the word "chair" as an example. It is a word used to label a concept. There are many objects that differ one from another, all of which are called chairs. Chairs are high and low, large and small, heavy and light, expensive and cheap, hard and soft, and so on. They are made of different types of materials (wood, metal, stone); they are used in many different places and for many different purposes; they have a varying number of legs; and they have or lack arms. The fact of the matter is, we could have a very large warehouse filled with chairs, no two of which would be alike, yet each would be called a "chair." Then again, think of the infinite variety we find among people, yet each one is called a "person."

In all the different chairs that we have experienced in our lifetime, there is something that we have found that they all have in common from the standpoint of use, namely, they are to be sat on. In whatever ways they differ, they have this in common, and it is this quality that we have in mind when we say that an object is a chair. *Concept formation,* therefore, *is a process of abstracting out of our many experiences that which they have in common.* When we do this we are again *discovering new relationships.*

In history books you have read about the many wars that men have fought; in social-studies texts you have read about the problems of production, distribution and consumption of goods; in newspapers you have read extensively about industrial strikes and collective bargaining. As a result of all this reading, have you discovered those *significant relationships* that give you insight into the causes of international conflicts, the nature of economic life, and the factors in industrial relations? If you have established some of these concepts, you have learned something that will give you greater insight when dealing with these aspects of our society in the future.

Conceptual learning also operates in the more immediate things of life that we are concerned about. There are the several different algebra problems that we solve and in which we find the operation of a general principle. There are the repeated experiences that we have with our roommate, or with a brother or a sister, in whom we begin to see certain traits and, hence, have more insight into the psychology of the other people with whom we are in intimate contact. There are the problems of grammar and of spelling in which we discover the rules of grammar and spelling. It is this type of discovery that we must seek in all the experiences that we have, for this process of discovery is the very essence of learning.

## INTERFERENCE WITH LEARNING

### Learning and Forgetting

*Forgetting is essential to learning.* Again and again you have deplored the fact that you forget so many things, especially during a test or final examination. Often you have wished that you had the power never to forget a thing. Actually, this would not be as desirable as you may think, for you would remember all the disagreeable things that you have experienced, and all the wrong things that you have learned, as well as the good and the correct things.

Suppose that back in the elementary grades you had learned that seven plus nine equals fifteen and that the word siege is spelled s-e-i-g-e, and you could *never* forget either of these incorrect responses. If this were the case, you would have a great deal of trouble each time you encountered the number combination "seven plus nine," or the word "siege." It is fortunate that you have forgotten these and many other incorrect responses you have learned in the past. Without forgetting, the learning of new things would be greatly hampered, if not completely impossible. Sometimes, therefore, it is good to forget. The regrettable part of forgetting is that we forget many desirable things that we wish to remember, as well as those that we wish to forget.

*Forgetting is characteristic.* Whether we want to or not, we do forget. Everyone forgets; it is characteristic of all of us. Moreover, we not only forget, but we forget more in the beginning than we do later; we forget more immediately after learning than we do after a lapse of time. You will forget more of what you have read in this chapter within the next hour or two than you will later today or tomorrow. When the results of forgetting are plotted on a curve, we call it the "forgetting curve."

This chapter contains fifteen secondary divisions distributed under the six primary divisions of the chapter. Each of these fifteen divisions has a heading in bold type at the left of the page, like the one that heads this section: "Learning and Forgetting." Below, you will find the complete outline of this chapter with the fifteen divisions numbered. Let us suppose that immediately after reading this chapter you will be able to give the *essential ideas* in each of these fifteen divisions; in other words, you will *know* the content of this chapter. Tomorrow, without reviewing the chapter, try again to recall the essential ideas in each division. What

you will find, in all probability, is that the content of
some of the divisions will be extremely vague, whereas the
content of others will be remembered clearly. You may say,
"I remember reading this section, but I can't remember what

## OUTLINE OF THIS CHAPTER

Live and Learn
  1. Learning Is Characteristic of All Life
  2. One Never Stops Learning
  3. The Need for Learning
The Definition of Learning
  4. Modification of Behavior
  5. Learning and Improvement
Trial-and-Error Learning
  6. A Primitive Type of Learning
  7. Factors Involved
  8. The Lazy Learner
Learning as Reproduction
  9. Rote Learning
  10. Memorization
Learning as Discovery
  11. Seeing New Relations
  12. Conceptual Learning
Interference with Learning
  13. Learning and Forgetting
  14. Learning and Emotion
  15. Learning and Attending

was discussed." The following day, follow through the outline again without rereading the chapter, as you did the day
before, and note how many of the divisions have little or no
meaning for you. Do this for four or five consecutive days.
If you follow through diligently on this little experiment and

*Learn More with Less Effort*

plot the results as in Figure 17, you will, in all probability, have a rather typical forgetting curve that will resemble the one in Figure 17.

Although forgetting is characteristic, and the trend in for-

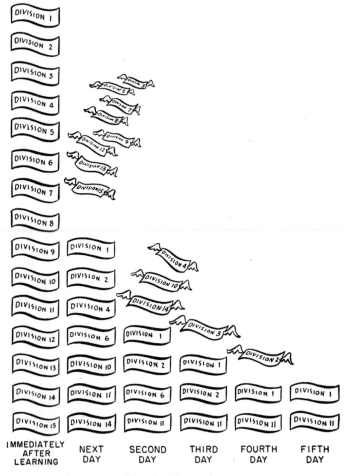

FIGURE 17. The Forgetting Curve.

getting is characteristic (forgetting most at the beginning and less and less later), *the amount of forgetting can be reduced.* Nothing will be gained, however, if we resign ourselves to the fact that forgetting is characteristic and do nothing about it. Because we forget much of what we desire to remember, we must do those things that will reduce substantially the amount of our forgetting. The several ways in which this can be done will be discussed extensively in the next two chapters.

*Why we forget.* Generally people attribute their forgetting either to the *lapse of time* or to *disuse.* Some people say, "It is so long since I thought about that, that I just can't remember it." Others give as their reason, "I have never needed that bit of information and so I don't remember it now." Both of these reasons are inadequate. A moment's reflection does reveal that we do recall things that we have not thought about for a long time. In fact, some very old people in their eighties and nineties do remember some incidents which date back to their early childhood and which have not been recalled but a very few times, if at all, in those eighty or ninety years. Time and lack of use are not the chief causes of forgetting; if they were, nothing that happened long ago or was not used for a long time would be remembered.

Psychological research points to another factor as the cause of forgetting. It is called "retroactive inhibition." What does this term mean? It means that *later experiences have an inhibitory effect on the retention of earlier experiences.* We forget yesterday's events, not just because they occurred yesterday, but because *we have experienced many events since then.* How do we know this? Two types of experiments point to retroactive inhibition as the cause of forgetting.

In the one type of experiment,[6] subjects memorize certain

---

[6] For a typical experiment see J. A. McGeoch and W. T. McDonald,

materials for a period of time and then follow that period
with another period during which they either learn material
very similar to that originally learned, learn very different
material, learn nothing (rest), or participate in some entirely
different activity (sing popular songs). At the close of the
second period (the period of interpolated material), their
retention is measured in any one of several ways (recall,
recognition, relearning). In this way, the effect of the interpolated material (similar material, different material, no
learning, dissimilar activity) on the recall of that which was
originally learned is measured. Experiments such as these
indicate that *the greater the similarity of the interpolated
material to the material originally learned the greater the
forgetting.* In other words, what one does, learns, or experiences *after* learning has an effect on the retention of that
which was learned earlier. See Figure 18 for a graphic rep-
resentation of this type of experiment.

A second, and similar, type of experiment [7] indicates that
forgetting after sleep is substantially less than the forgetting
that occurs during waking life which is filled with experience.

These experiments must not be interpreted to mean that
after learning something we should sleep until the moment
we have need for it; rather, they indicate that care needs to
be exercised in the type of activity that follows learning. If
we follow the study of French vocabularies with the study of
Spanish vocabularies, we are headed for trouble. Therefore,
let us order our study procedure so that whatever activity

---

"Meaningful Relation and Retroactive Inhibition," *American Journal
of Psychology,* 1931, *43:* 579–588.

[7] J. G. Jenkins and K. M. Dallenbach, "Obliviscence during sleep
and waking," *Journal of Psychology,* 1924, *35:* 605–612; E. B. Van
Ormer, "Retention after intervals of sleep and waking," *Archives of
Psychology,* New York, 1932, No. 137.

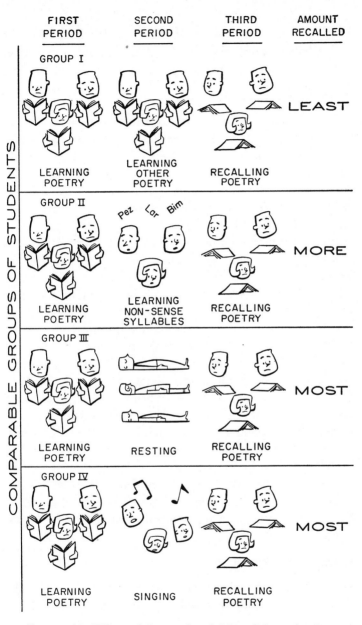

| FIRST PERIOD | SECOND PERIOD | THIRD PERIOD | AMOUNT RECALLED |
|---|---|---|---|

GROUP I

LEARNING POETRY | LEARNING OTHER POETRY | RECALLING POETRY | LEAST

GROUP II

Pez Lar Bim

LEARNING POETRY | LEARNING NON-SENSE SYLLABLES | RECALLING POETRY | MORE

GROUP III

LEARNING POETRY | RESTING | RECALLING POETRY | MOST

GROUP IV

LEARNING POETRY | SINGING | RECALLING POETRY | MOST

COMPARABLE GROUPS OF STUDENTS

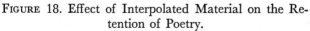

FIGURE 18. Effect of Interpolated Material on the Retention of Poetry.

which follows a learning period will have as little retroactive effect as possible on what has just been learned.

## Learning and Emotion

That emotion hampers recall of what has been learned is apparent to everyone. After a perfectly adequate preparation of an assignment, you have found yourself unable to recall that which you studied and to recite adequately in class because, being called on unexpectedly, you were exceedingly self-conscious. At various times, you have been unable to recall immediately certain facts needed to answer an examination question because of fear of failure. When fear grips you, you are generally unable to think of anything. We have all seen a person stand before an audience and be so overcome with fear that he was unable to speak—sometimes a person cannot even recall his own name under these circumstances. This is what fear and self-consciousness do to us!

Emotion not only hampers recall of that which has been learned; it also interferes with the learning of new knowledge and of new skills. Unpleasant emotions are accompanied by tension, anxiety, and frustration. When we are tense, anxious, and frustrated, we are incapable of maintaining sustained attention, preserving a critical attitude, and using sagacious judgment, all of which are essential to effective learning. Emotional behavior is essentially primitive behavior that is random in nature, whereas learning demands controlled responses. Therefore, emotion, and especially unpleasant emotion, must be kept at a minimum if learning is to be facilitated.

## Learning and Attending

Only seconds remain in the game; your team has the ball; that last crucial play that will determine the victor is about to be made. Your eyes are glued to the ball and the player who holds it. You are wholly unaware of everything else around you. You are thinking only one thing: Make it! Make it! This is attention at its highest. How long can you maintain this degree of concentration? You can maintain it only for a very short time at your very best, and then you will shift to something else. One never attends to one thing for long; one constantly shifts from one thing to another. This is the nature of attention. Even sustained attention is not without fluctuation. In sustained attention, however, we come back again and again to the same idea or object of attention with but very brief deviations from it.

Why is it that we are unable to attend continuously without wavering? The reason is: being living organisms, which means that we are constantly active, we cannot maintain a given set or adjustment except for a short period of time. As the result of our activity, we get out of adjustment; and when we are out of adjustment to something we are not attending to it. When we attend, we come into the best possible relationship with the stimulus; but since this best adjustment cannot be maintained for long, we must constantly *readjust* to that which we are reading or studying in order to maintain a high degree of attention. We must establish *the habit of constantly readjusting* to that which we are studying so that our attention will be sustained. Without sustained attention, we gain little from our school work. Keep the level of attention high; learn more with less effort!

# 4.

# The Techniques of Effective Learning

## CONFUSION OF RITUAL WITH LEARNING

### Types of Ritual

Ritual plays a rather important part in the life of each of us. There are fraternity and sorority rituals, rituals in honor societies and clubs, rituals in school organizations and church services. A ritual, psychologically speaking, is a series of well-established habits that show an attitude of submission to authority and which are believed to accomplish something with reference to one's future status, success, or achievement. A ritual, therefore, is generally a preliminary to something else. Not infrequently, this preliminary (the ritual) comes to be substituted for that to which it is a preliminary and, therefore, comes to be an end in itself. Some people even regard a ritual as a sort of magical performance that can be substituted for the more stern demands of life to which the ritual is intended to introduce us.

Ritual is a part of our personal lives as well as of our group activities. Our personal rituals which may be less formal and more individual than our group rituals are just as firmly established (if not more so), are just as compelling, are followed just as blindly, and are believed to be just as magical. This is certainly true of the many rituals students indulge in as preliminaries to studying. Let us see what some of these prestudy rituals are.

*Personal rituals.* Some of the rituals indulged in as preliminary to studying are of a very personal sort. There is the student who must go through the ritual of dressing for the ordeal of evening study. He rolls up his shirt sleeves or dons a smoking jacket, puts on bedroom slippers, smokes a cigarette, sharpens all his pencils, listens to a sports broadcast followed by a news cast and the weather report, cleans his several pipes, and scratches his scalp free of dandruff—all before he can settle down to studying.

A girl, on the other hand, may follow the ritual of slipping into a housecoat before studying, putting her hair up in pin curls, manicuring her nails, removing the day's make-up, rereading the last five letters received from her boy friend, and doodling for ten minutes or longer on the desk blotter while contemplating dreamily the boy friend's picture—all before serious study is begun.

*Gastronomical ritual.* Some students' prestudy ritual takes the form of eating. They reinspect the box that arrived several days ago from home containing choice things prepared by mother, and which they know has been cleaned of crumbs at least forty-eight hours ago. Finding the box empty, they inspect their roommate's box with the intention of purloining a snack from it, but alas, it too is empty! Eat they must, so they sample an apple, down a bottle of coke, eat a candy bar, and perhaps end up at the corner drug store where they polish off a Dagwood sandwich! They need energy to study,

PERSONAL
RITUAL

GASTRO-
NOMICAL
RITUAL

SOCIAL
RITUAL

FIGURE 19. Types of Prestudy Ritual.

they say. This, however, they do each evening before attempting to study and to prepare their assignments for the next day.

*Social ritual.* Then there are those students who may neither eat nor attend to personal things before studying, but who find many social obligations that seem to be particularly pressing before studying can be done. They *must* talk to someone in a distant part of the dormitory, stopping on the way when both going and coming to see several other people. Then there are the telephone calls that must be made, calls which are postponed again and again because of one's inability to get the line, or the right party after the line has been gotten. Unable to complete their call, they can think of nothing better to do than to sit by the telephone fuming and verbalizing their frustration which they attribute to the poor service given by the telephone company.

## The Psychology of Prestudy Ritual

Why do students indulge in these prestudy rituals? Examine your own motivation when you indulge in ritualistic activities and see what you find. Chances are you will defend some or all of these activities as both legitimate and necessary, as so many of them are, but why do you find them so necessary just prior to studying? If you are perfectly honest with yourself and face the issue squarely, you will probably admit that more time, perhaps much more time, is spent on these ritualistic activities than is necessary, simply because they afford a seemingly legitimate reason for postponing studying—studying that is anticipated as being both difficult and disagreeable. Admit to yourself that you cannot bear the thought of getting down to the *work* of studying and therefore fritter away your time in ritualistic activities that you are constantly reassuring yourself are essential.

A second attitude toward prestudy ritual is this: since

ritual is considered an essential preliminary to studying, it is made a part of the activity of studying itself. Therefore, time spent on ritual is regarded as time spent studying. In fact, some students spend so much time on ritualistic performances that they have little or no time left for actual study. Yet, when they are questioned as to the amount of time spent on an assignment inadequately prepared, they affirm that they *did study,* that they studied the *whole evening.* Time spent is not synonymous with studying. Do not count study time as beginning with the pronouncement, "Now I shall study my math," if this assertion of intention is separated from the solution of the first problem by many minutes, or even one or several hours, of ritualistic activities.

Be realistic! Recognize prestudy ritual for what it is. Know that rituals are attempts to postpone what you are not at all eager to do, and that these activities are not to be confused with studying. If you are seeking to learn more with less effort, cut the ritual! Get on with the work!

## METHODS OF ATTACK IN LEARNING

There are right ways and wrong ways, effective and efficient, and ineffective and wasteful ways, of doing anything. Allowing a person to do something in his own way does not mean that he will discover the most effective and efficient way of doing the task. Even after much time and experience with the task, it does not mean that his method of dealing with it will be the best—in fact it may not even be acceptable.

You have been at the task of studying for what seems to you a very long time. Yet, you may not know how to learn efficiently. The purpose of this and the following chapter is to point out to you a number of methods of attack on the matter of effective learning. Each of the methods presented here is not of the same importance or effectiveness as every other method. Moreover, they are not interchangeable; that is, one cannot be substituted for another. Some are limited to certain kinds of learning; others can be used only with certain types of materials. Neither are they all equally valuable from the standpoint of the returns they give in effective learning. However, they are ways that have been found to have more or less value for others and they will help you also to learn more with less effort after you learn when and where to use them. Study each technique carefully. Learn *how* and *when* to use each. Know what each will accomplish for you. Make these techniques so much a part of you that they will be as familiar as eating and dressing. Having become familiar with them, *use them at every opportunity*.

## THE STUDY-REST-STUDY-REST METHOD

### The Psychology of Distributed Learning

The study-rest-study-rest method of learning is generally known as the *spaced method* because practices or learning periods are *distributed in time* separated by periods of rest or by periods of very different activity. This method is generally contrasted with the method of continuous study usually known (at least prior to an examination) as *cramming*. Psychological studies have shown repeatedly that spaced or distributed learning is superior to concentrated, one-period learning. There are a number of reasons for this.

Spaced learning means that one returns to the same material a number of times. As one does return to the same material, different portions of it have different attention value on the several occasions. Hence, that which was not attended to and passed unnoticed during an earlier study period may be attended to during the later study period. This is logical in

FIGURE 20. Spaced Learning.

view of what was said earlier about the fluctuation of attention. Often a fact or idea "hits" us differently when encountered the second time than it does on our first contact with it. Therefore, by returning to the same material more than once, we give ourselves the opportunity to experience that which is being learned in more than one way—an opportunity we are much less likely to have when our learning is concentrated.

Furthermore, spaced learning generally means that we spend more time studying than we do when it is confined to one period only, and by spending more time we give ourselves the opportunity to learn more or to learn it more thoroughly. Students rarely spend too much time studying; frequently they spend too little. Since spaced learning encourages one to spend more time, it is a good technique to use.

By breaking off learning and returning to it a number of times, one experiences less fatigue because the learning is broken off, when fatigue begins to set in, with the confidence that the learning will be completed at a later time. When, on the other hand, the student feels that he must complete his learning at one sitting, he forces himself, in spite of fatigue, to continue. Learning under these conditions is much less apt to be rewarding.

The rest pause following a period of learning gives one an opportunity to integrate that which is learned. There seems to be a tendency, not too well understood, to do this. Each of us has experienced this tendency to perseverate when we have tried repeatedly, and without success, to solve a mathematical problem, only to find the solution easily the next morning. Something seems to happen during sleep (a rest pause) so that we are able to integrate the elements of the problem differently the next morning and so discover the solution easily. The use of the study-rest-study-rest method gives us the opportunity to have this experience more often.

The rest pause not only makes integration possible; it also makes forgetting possible. We pointed out above the importance of forgetting. During the rest-pauses, the wrong things which are learned are forgotten, thus making retention of the right things more likely.

### Some General Principles

With these advantages of the spaced method in mind, let us turn to another matter, namely, the *length of the practice or study period*. No specific rules can be set down, but a few guiding principles should be noted. In the case of the older student who is learning complex material such as is found in college-level subjects, the learning period needs to be longer. That is, one should not expect to be on a five- to seven-minute schedule, appropriate for a primary-grade child, when one is studying algebra or trigonometry in college. In these latter instances, both the complexity of the subject and the age of the learner demand longer study periods of forty-five to ninety minutes and more. There is a warm-up period in learning just as in athletics, and if the learning period is too short, one never gets beyond the warm-up stage. In the case of simple learning in which there is a great deal of repetition, or as in the establishment of simpler skills, shorter practice periods a few minutes in duration, followed by short rest periods, seem to be more effective.

Perhaps a good rule to follow is to continue a learning period as long as motivation is strong and attention is sustained. When one finds that it takes increasing effort to drive oneself to continue and attention fluctuates extensively, then it is time to take a rest pause.

How long should a rest pause be? Here again, there is no

infallible rule to follow. Generally, the length of the rest pause is determined somewhat by the length of the working period. A longer working period demands a longer rest pause and a short one can be followed by a short rest pause. When learning skills, short work periods followed by short rest pauses seem to result in greater efficiency.

Finally, what about the nature of one's activity when on a rest pause? A rest pause does not necessarily mean *no* activity; essentially it means a change in activity. A change from academic learning (history) to learning a skill (piano practice) with a later return to the academic subject is an illustration of how the distributed method can be used. Even a change from one academic subject to another may be effective. Follow a period of literature study with a period of learning chemical symbols or formulas; rest by typing a term paper after studying psychology. Even in studying the same subject, the rest period can be introduced by making biological drawings or preparing an insect collection after memorizing biological classifications. In any case, what is done during the rest period should be as different from what was done during the study period as possible. The essential reason for this is that it will give rise to a minimum of forgetting due to retroactive inhibition.

The study-rest-study-rest method of learning is highly recommended. Give it a fair trial!

## PUT IT INTO WORDS

Ask a fellow student to give you the meanings of some common words such as "personality," or "freedom," or "intelligence." Suppose you ask your roommate, "Do you know what personality is?" "Sure I know," will be his prompt reply. "Well, just what is it?" you ask inquiringly. "Well," he begins, "personality . . . personality? . . . yes, personality is . . . it is . . . well, when you have it, you are popular." From this vague statement would you say that your fellow student *knows* what personality is? Hardly! Give him, or some of your other friends, other equally common words, such as "box" and "chair," and discover for yourself what little content common words have for many people. Better yet, try to state what *you* mean by some of these common words and see whether you do any better than your friends. Each of you is apt to say, "Yes, I know the word 'personality.'" But what do you really mean when you say you *know* a word? Do you mean that you have *heard* it; that you can *pronounce* it; that you can *use* it in a sentence; or that you *know* its meaning?

There is a difference between being *familiar* with a word and *knowing* its meaning. Do not confuse the two. Why is it that so many people are just *familiar* with words? The answer is: they fail to attempt to define words in terms of other words that are meaningful to them. They are satisfied with a vague sort of feeling that they know the word and they never test themselves by attempting to define it. To know something well one must put it into words. Verbalizing facilitates learning. This is as true of learning skills as of learning ideational material.

Experimental evidence supports the above generalizations. In one such experiment,[1] fifth-grade children learned to assemble a three-dimensional cross puzzle from six oblong blocks, five of which interlocked with each other in one way only and the sixth locked the whole cross holding the parts together firmly (see Figure 21). Four groups of 25 children each were used. The children in the first group were required to count by two's to 100 while watching the experimenter

[1] Louise Thompson, unpublished report described by M. May, "The Psychology of Learning from Demonstration Films," *Journal of Educational Psychology,* 1946, *37*:1–12.

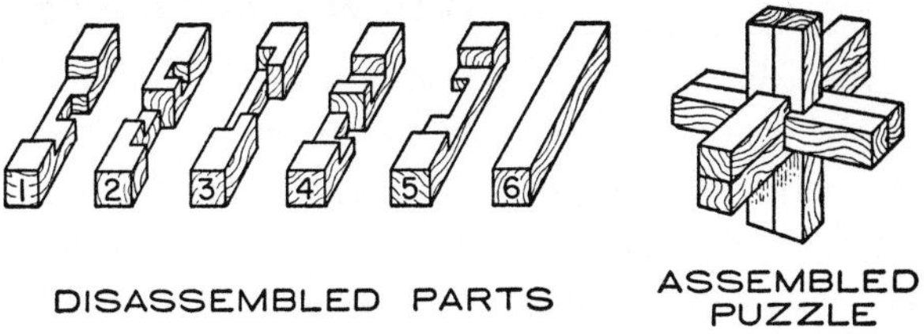


| | NUMBER OF CHILDREN | ACTIVITY | | CHILDREN WHO LEARNED | AVERAGE NUMBER OF TRIALS |
|---|---|---|---|---|---|
| GROUP I | 25 | CHILD COUNTING | 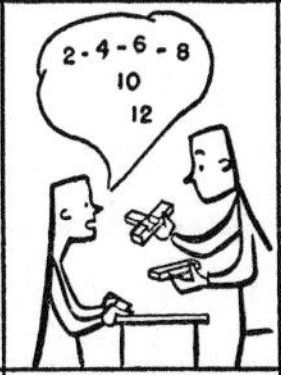  | 3 | – |
| GROUP II | 25 | CHILD DESCRIBING | 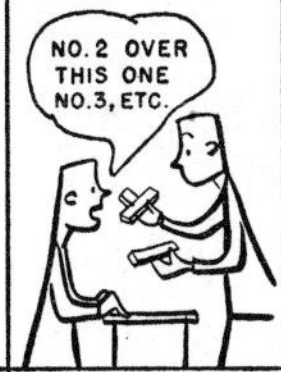  | 22 | 16 |
| GROUP III | 25 | EXPERIMENTER DESCRIBING | 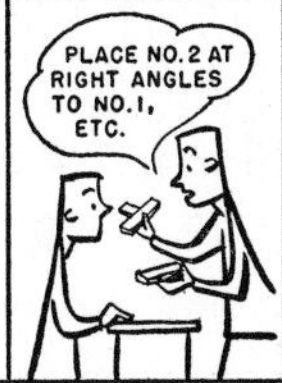  | 25 | 14 |
| GROUP IV | 25 | CHILD DESCRIBING, EXPERIMENTER CORRECTING | 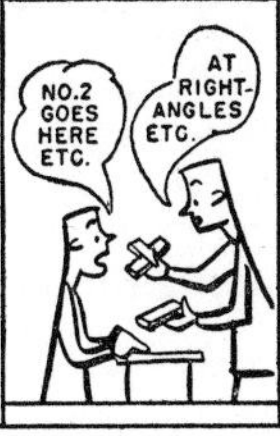  | 25 | 12 |

FIGURE 21. Importance of Verbalization in Learning to Assemble a Three-Dimensional Cross Puzzle. (Data adapted from M. May, "The Psychology of Learning from Demonstrational Films," *Jour. Educ. Psych.*, 1946, *37*: 1–12. Used with the permission of Warwick and York, Publishers.)

demonstrate the steps in the assembly of the puzzle. Only three of the 25 children learned by this method. Each *child* in the second group *described* the demonstrator's actions as he progressed with the demonstration. Twenty-two of the 25 children learned in an average of 16 trials. The children in the third group remained silent while the *demonstrator described* the steps in the assembly of the puzzle. By this method, all 25 children learned in an average of 14 trials. The *children* in the fourth group *described* the steps in the assembly of the puzzle as they were demonstrated by the experimenter and were *corrected in their description* by the demonstrator. Not only did all 25 children in this group learn; they learned in an average of only 12 trials.

Note that when the children were engaged in another activity (counting by two's) almost none learned. However, nearly all learned when they verbalized the steps in the assembly, but it took them longer (average of 16 trials) because their *verbalized descriptions were not adequate*. All learned, and more quickly (average of 14 trials), when the *demonstrator described in a very adequate way* the steps required. The demonstrator's superior description of the steps taken (superior to the children's descriptions in Group II) facilitated their learning. The children in Group IV learned still more quickly (12 trials) because *they described* and the *demonstrator corrected* their descriptions (showed them how to state it better) as they went along, thus assuring a superior description of the steps in the process of the assembly of the puzzle.

These results demonstrate rather well the importance of *stating* carefully (putting into words) that which one is learning. Moreover, the results of this experiment indicate that those children who were *poor in describing were slow in learning,* and those who were *fast learners were superior in giving verbal accounts* of their activities.

*Improve the quality of your learning by putting that which you learn into words.* Increase your vocabulary so that you will be better able to do this, and establish the set of putting everything you attempt to learn into meaningful words.

In another experiment,[2] college students were comparing varying lengths of a bar with a standard length on an instrument called a Galton Bar. In one part of the experiment, the subjects were required to guess the magnitude of their error as well as be punished if their error in judgment exceeded a certain fixed amount. Guessing forced the subjects to *put into* words the nature of their error, and this verbalization enabled the subjects to earn the best scores when this was done— better scores than when any of the following was used: punishment alone, reward, punishment with information given, or knowledge of results. Putting one's activities into words enables one to achieve more.

Try the following experiment and see how verbalization really works. Figure 22 presents the results of a learning experiment in which several groups of rats learned the pattern of an elevated maze. Without knowing any more about the experiment than this, turn now to Figure 22 and study it for just *one minute,* then close your book and try to recall what you saw and what it means.

Now return to Figure 22 and start talking about it. Put what you see into words and write down as many observations as you can. What are some of the things that you can *say* about Figure 22? Here are some of the things that you should say: (1) the left margin of the graph indicates the average errors committed, and (2) the base line indicates the

---

[2] H. C. Hamilton, "The Effect of Incentives on Accuracy of Discrimination," *Archives of Psychology,* New York, 1929, No. 103.

number of trials or runs made; (3) five groups of rats were
used in the experiment; (4) normal animals did much better
than those deprived of one or more senses; (5) animals de-

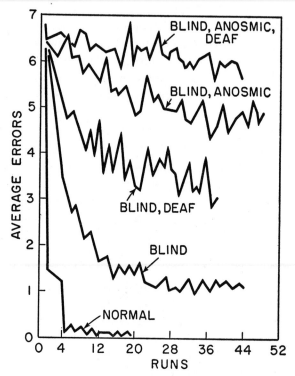

FIGURE 22. Sensory Deprivation and Maze Learning in
White Rats. (Adapted from C. H. Honzik, *The Sen-
sory Basis of Maze Learning in Rats*, in *Comparative
Psychology Monographs*, 1936, *13*: No. 64.)

prived of one sense (sight) were handicapped less than those
deprived of two or three senses; (6) the loss of the sense of
smell (anosmic) handicapped the rats more than deafness,
since the blind and anosmic rats did more poorly than the

blind and deaf rats did; (7) the maze problem must have been simple, since normal animals learned it almost to perfection in four trials; (8) rats deprived of three senses show practically no learning whatsoever; (9) the blind-deaf rats were run for fewer trials than the other three handicapped groups were. Now close your book and put away your list and see how many of these observations that you have put into words you can remember. Three things are, in all probability, evident from this little experiment: you made more observations by verbalizing; you know definitely how many observations you made and what they are; and finally, you remember them more vividly. These are the gains that come from putting what one is learning into words.

## USE SEVERAL SENSES

Return again to Figure 22 and note what the results indicate. They show clearly that the loss of one or several senses handicapped the animals in maze learning, and that the greater the sensory handicap the greater the loss in learning ability. If the inability to use certain senses decreases learning ability, then the reverse should also be true. Therefore, we can say that the more senses we use, the more effective and extensive our learning will be.

All of our knowledge of the world around us comes from our senses. We are not born with certain ideas as some of the ancients thought. It is quite obvious that a person born blind can never know the beauty of a sunset; the person born deaf can never learn to play the piano; and the anosmic person (without a sense of smell) can never become a discriminating tea or coffee taster. Certain senses are essential to the learning of certain things; they give us cues to which to respond. The more varied the sensory cues to which we respond, the more complex is the learning of which we are capable. Thus, one

SEE IT

 SAY IT

 HEAR IT

 DRAW OR WRITE IT

FIGURE 23. Learn More by Seeing, Hearing, and Doing.

of the secrets of effective learning is to *employ as many senses as possible* and to respond to as many sensory cues as one can.

That the use of several senses does facilitate learning has been brought home to you by audio-visual aids. You know that when you *see* and *hear* a sound movie, a television program, or a demonstration of some kind, you learn more and remember longer what you learn than when you read about the same things in a textbook. The reason you learn more and remember it longer is that you are having *two different contacts* (sight and hearing) with the material at the same time. The various sensory experiences supplement each other; there are more opportunities for associations to be established. Ideas become more real and dynamic. They also seem more natural, and they are more natural because you always experience many sensations at the same time. We do not just see or just hear; we *see and hear* at the same time. When learning, let us do it the natural way—the way in which we *use several senses at once.*

But how can we use several senses at once when we are learning, and how will their use help us to learn more? Most students think of studying in terms of reading an assignment. Reading, as you have been taught it, is a visual activity. This is as it should be; you should use only your eyes when reading silently. This type of reading makes for rapid reading and rapid reading generally increases comprehension. Silent reading, then, which is visual reading, has very definite advantages and no one familiar with education would advocate that you become a lip reader. Nevertheless, silent reading, if used as the sole avenue of approach to that which is being learned, limits one to a single means of contact with the subject matter. It is as if you saw a movie from which the sound track has been removed. Would you enjoy this type of movie? Would it be realistic? Would you learn much from it, if it

were an educational film? Just as the movie becomes more
enjoyable when the pictures are supplemented by sound, so
material that is being studied and learned becomes more
meaningful and interesting when other sensory experiences
supplement the visual ones.

When studying school subjects, three senses should be
used. *Sight* and *hearing* have already been emphasized. Add
to these the *kinesthetic sense.* The kinesthetic sense, of which
you probably are unaware, is a sense on which you rely constantly. Kinesthetic sensations are those that come from the
movement of muscles and joints and which are essential to
every motor response that you make. None of the coördinated
responses, the skills, of which you are capable would be possible without kinesthetic sensitivity. Kinesthetic sensations are
the cues to motor responses; they are also the cues that can
be used in learning. We can use them by making use of motor
activity when learning. Return once more to Figure 22. Examine it carefully and then draw (not trace) on a sheet of
paper this graph so that you duplicate this figure as accurately as possible. After drawing it by following the figure in
the book, close the book and draw it from memory. Compare
your drawing with the original, correct it if it differs from
the one in the book, and then try again to reproduce it from
memory. When you finish doing this, you will *know* the figure
and the story that it tells.

This technique, therefore, prescribes that you *see* (read
silently) what you are learning; that you *hear* it by talking
about it, by telling or explaining it to someone else (put it
into words);[3] and that you *draw* or *write it out* so that
motor sensations are used.

Use this simple formula:

[3] See pp. 89–95.

SEE IT, SAY IT, HEAR IT, DO IT

Once you become accustomed to doing this, you will find it easy, and dividends in terms of material learned will be high.

## SETTING IMMEDIATE GOALS

### The Psychology of Goals

Goals, like targets, are things we shoot at. Because a goal is something that we shoot at, it *gives direction* to our activity and response. But goals do more than give direction to our activity; they, so to speak, *compel us to act,* not because they exert any mysterious power over us, but because *we* respond to them positively. This compelling power (called "positive valence" by some psychologists) is not in the goal; rather it is in us. It is not that *it* attracts us, as much as *we* are attracted to it. Unless we are attracted to something so that we try to achieve it, that something is not a goal. Another common observation is that we are attracted more strongly to some goals than to others—some are more compelling than others. Moreover, some goals are immediate and others are remote; some are achievable almost immediately or in the very near future, while others are remote in time.

Generally speaking, remote goals are much less compelling as to our present activity than immediate goals are. The goal of passing a test tomorrow stirs us to action today far more effectively than the goal of passing comprehensive examinations for graduation three or four years from now. We feel the necessity of action when the goal is immediate; we console ourselves that there is plenty of time when the goal is remote. When the goal is immediate and pressing, we say, "I must act now or fail"; but when it is remote, we think, "Yes, yes, someday I shall . . ."

The final point with regard to the psychology of immediate

FIGURE 24. Get into the Magnetic Field of an Immediate Goal.

goals is that this technique increases tremendously the incidence of satisfaction and pleasure. Each time we achieve an immediate goal we experience the thrill of achievement which is pleasurable. Since the goals are immediate, they are achieved in rather close succession, thus giving rise to the experience of pleasure again and again. Each time we achieve, we are eager to "try it again," and each additional time we are successful the stronger our drive to continue becomes. Hence, we progress step by step, each step a new satisfaction, until ultimately we reach the more remote goal that was not sufficiently strong to motivate us in the beginning. Give the psychology of immediate goals the chance to operate in you. Get into the goal's field of force! Be active! Enjoy the satisfaction of achievement!

## How to Use Immediate Goals

There are two specific ways in which we can make use of immediate goals when learning school subjects or mastering skills. The first of these has to do with the material, and the second with time.

*Set a quota.* Suppose that someone hiring you as a typist told you that during your first year of employment you had to make 15,625,000 strokes on the typewriter. Would you take the job? Chances are you would gasp: "Over 15 million strokes! No, thank you. I could never do that." The goal of making 15,625,000 strokes on the typewriter would overwhelm you. Since you refuse the job, let us suppose that your prospective employer revises his proposition so that you will be required to type 3,125,000 words during the year. This too seems enormous to you and hence very discouraging. Because you are still not sold on the job, the employer now sets the year's goal at 12,500 letters of about 250 words each. This you may be willing to consider, but the number still remains unbelievably large. Finally, the employer gives you his final proposition, namely, that you type one letter (average of 250 words) each 9.6 minutes of a 40-hour week during a 50-week year. At your speed of 60 words per minute, you can type a 250-word letter in less than $4\frac{1}{2}$ minutes, and so actually you will be resting half of the time each day that you are on the job. One letter in a little less than 10 minutes! Yes, you can do that. You assure your prospective employer that you are interested in his proposition, and take the job willingly.

Now figure it all out for yourself. Fifty letters per day for 50 40-hour weeks makes a total of 12,500 letters per year. If each letter contains, on the average, 250 words, you will type 3,125,000 words, and if each word averages 5 letters, you will type a grand total of 15,625,000 strokes during the year and still be resting half of the time!

When the goal is remote (number of strokes per year), attainment is so far away that we even refuse to consider the job, let alone try to achieve its completion. On the other hand, when the goal is immediate (one letter per 9.6 minutes), we accept it and having reached it, we set a new immediate goal, followed by another immediate goal, and sometimes, almost before we know it, we arrive at the more remote goal to which all the immediate goals lead.

Therefore, one way to use immediate goals is to set achievable quotas that are close enough to be compelling. As a typist, set for yourself the goal of averaging one letter each ten minutes or six an hour not 12,500 per year. When studying school subjects, *set for yourself the goal of reading so many pages* in the text (perhaps 30 or 40, or only 10 or 15) *before you will stop*. After you attain your first goal of 30 pages, set another immediate goal of reading the remaining 17 in the chapter. Of the 35 problems in algebra that you

# SET A QUOTA—

TYPE THREE PAGES
BEFORE CLASS

TYPE FOUR
PAGES
AFTER LUNCH

TYPE LAST
SIX PAGES
BEFORE DINNER

FIGURE 25. Set a Quota that Can Be Reached in the
Immediate Future.

must solve, set the immediate goal of solving 12 now. When the first 12 are solved, set another immediate goal of solving another 10. By doing this, you will have all of them solved sooner than you think, and with much more satisfaction and much less annoyance.

In any task that you undertake, set a quota that you *can reach early.* As a result of reaching it early, you will derive considerable satisfaction and pleasure. Because you are pleased with your success in doing what you set out to do, it is easier to set another goal which, when achieved, will likewise give you pleasure—the kind of pleasure you have had again and again when you said, "I'm glad that is done!" The experience of pleasure stimulates one to attempt the achievement of another goal, and before you know it the whole job is done. Try this out for yourself and prove that it is true!

*Work against the clock.* A second way to employ the technique of immediate goals is to work against the clock. This is similar to the technique of setting quotas for yourself; the difference is that you are now thinking in terms of time instead of in terms of amount of material learned. Let us see how this technique works.

You have 30 or 60 minutes of time, in which you can study. You may, of course, think: "What is 30 minutes; I can't accomplish anything in that short period of time." Hence, you waste the time and accomplish nothing. You may take the attitude that nothing worth while can be accomplished unless you have a large block of time—three or four hours. Too often, having the large block of time in which to study, you take the attitude that you have a great deal of time and so there is little need for putting on the pressure that results in effective learning. Consequently, it is not uncommon for a person to fritter away much of that large block of study time

# WORK AGAINST THE CLOCK

GOAL:
  THREE PARAGRAPHS
  OF GERMAN BY 9:30

FIGURE 26. Work Against the Clock.

with but little accomplished. This is inefficiency of a most objectionable sort.

Use the short periods of time that are available to you. Set an immediate goal that is appropriate for the amount of time you have available. Set the immediate goal of translating two or three paragraphs of your German assignment during the 30 minutes you have between classes. Set the immediate goal of solving at least three chemistry problems, or of copying a part of your literature notes, or of looking up in the dictionary those seven words that are unfamiliar to you, or memorize the first stanza of the poem assigned in English. True, no one of these immediate tasks when finished will be the whole assignment, but each will be a satisfactory beginning, and the fact that you make a beginning is as important as the fact that something has been accomplished.

Set the immediate goal of getting a certain amount done by a certain time, no matter how little time you have at your disposal. Set for yourself the goal of completing your assignment in biology by 8:30, your economics by 9:45, and your French by 11:00 with a break between the economics and the French. Be specific as to when you expect to complete a block of work. Set a definite time. Work to achieve your goal. Remember to be reasonable in the goals that you set for yourself.

Two rules need to be observed in the setting of immediate goals: (1) they must be achievable, at least most of the time; (2) they must be such as to exert a pressure on you, a pressure to keep you working. It is foolish to set a goal that is much less than that which you can achieve with some effort. Set a goal that can be reached, but also set one that "puts the screws" on you. *Keep your learning efficiency high by working against the clock.*

# 5.

## *The Techniques of Effective Learning (Continued)*

### USE RECITATION

#### The Meaning of Recitation

To some people the word "recitation" means a painful attempt to respond orally in a class situation to a teacher's or a professor's difficult and meaningless questions; to others, fortunately, it means a pleasurable experience of giving learned information to the members of a class. Recitation also means to some people the activity of repeating, somewhat mechanically, that which was memorized, generally by rote, such as poetry or the lines of a play. In any case, recitation is generally associated with questions, teachers, and classroom situations.

Recitation from the broader view of psychology means much more than this. *Recitation is any attempt to reproduce, in any way, that which is being (or has been) learned.* Recitation is not limited to the classroom; one can recite anywhere. Nor is it only a question-and-answer proposition. It is *any attempt* to reproduce that which one is learning. In the

section, "How to Recite," we shall discuss fully the several
ways in which one can recite.

FIGURE 27. Use Recitation.

## Recitation Is Effective

One does not really have to convince you of the value of recitation because you have used it to good advantage in some areas both in and outside of the classroom. For example, you are convinced that the best way to remember a good joke is to tell it a number of times to your friends, and after you have done so, you just cannot forget it. This process of *telling* the joke to your friends is nothing other than recitation. You know that recitation works with jokes; discover that it works with other learned things too. Certainly there is not one psychology for learning jokes and another psychology for learning material found in academic subjects. Learning is learning wherever we find it, and the psychology is the same even though that which is learned differs. Experimental evidence obtained in the psychology laboratory supports this view.

In one classic experiment on the value of recitation,[1] eighth-grade children used various amounts of reading and recitation in learning biographical material such as is found in *Who's Who*. One group spent all of their time reading and none reciting; a second group devoted 80 percent of their time to reading and 20 percent to reciting; a third group distributed their time on a 60 and 40 basis between reading and reciting; a fourth group used the distribution of 40 and 60; a fifth, of 20 and 80, and the sixth group spent only 10 percent of their time reading and 90 percent reciting. The results clearly indicate that in both immediate and delayed recall (after four hours) retention is greater when recitation is used. In fact, 40 or more percent of one's time can be spent in recitation with a substantial gain in the amount of material learned. When no recitation was used, 16 percent of the bio-

[1] A. I. Gates, "Recitation as a Factor in Memorizing," *Archives of Psychology*, New York, 1917, VI, No. 40.

graphical material was remembered after four hours; but when 40 percent or more time was spent on recitation, 25 or 26 percent of the material was remembered. This means that half again as much and more of the material was remembered when recitation was used as compared to what was remembered when no recitation, and only reading, was used.

Recruits at a reception center learning the "phonetic alphabet" that is used in army signals, learned from 6 to more than 27 percent more, depending on other conditions, when they used recitation.[2]

Similar results were obtained in experiments on the value of recitation in learning French vocabulary.[3] Studies in the learning of spelling and arithmetic from this point of view have yielded the same general results.[4]

*Reasons why recitation is effective.* (1) Recitation keeps motivation strong. When one is determined to recite what he is reading and learning, he keeps his attention on his work and strives to reach his goal. (2) Recitation facilitates the use of immediate goals. By the very fact that one looks forward to reproducing what he is now learning, he is setting an immediate goal. It is an *immediate* goal, for when one uses recitation he does not expect to recite after several days or weeks, but immediately following a learning period. (3) Recitation also tells us how well we are progressing in our learning. If we reproduce either well or poorly that which we are learning, we have a rough measure of our success in learning. (4) Recitation gives rise to reward when we are successful, or to punishment when we are much less successful in reproducing that which we are learning, and we all know

[2] C. I. Hovland, A. A. Lumsdaine, and F. D. Sheffield, *Experiments in Mass Communication*, Princeton: Princeton University Press, 1949.

[3] L. C. Seibert, "A series of experiments on the learning of French vocabulary," *Johns Hopkins Univ. Stud. Educ.*, 1932, No. 18.

[4] G. Forlano, "School learning with various methods of practice and rewards," *Teach. Coll. Contr. Educ.*, 1936, No. 688.

that reward and punishment (especially reward) facilitate learning. (5) Finally, recitation gives us practice in doing what we ultimately want to do. When we recite the poem we are learning, or the formulas in chemistry, or the definitions in psychology, or the factors involved in an historical event, we are doing the very thing that we expect to be able to do when we come to the final examination in the course, or up against a problem in our work later in life.

## How to Recite

Most people think of recitation as an audible or subvocal oral response, and so often it is, but there are other ways in which one can recite. True, much of the time you will *say it* because what you are learning is verbal material. However, you need not always say it; you may *write it*. This may be a little slower but it does utilize different senses and that, as we noted earlier, is a good thing to do. Some things lend themselves to drawing, and so *draw them*. If you are learning a complex electrical circuit in physics, the floor plan of an animal experiment in psychology, or some economic trends or data represented graphically, *draw them*. You will be surprised how effective this form of recitation can be in indicating knowledge or the lack of it.

One can also recite by using what we commonly think of as reproductive imagination. *Picture it*. See in your imagination that battlefield diagramed in your text; visualize the characteristics of each of the several types of architecture you are studying. If your auditory imagery is more vivid, use it. *Hear it*. Imagine you are hearing Lincoln delivering the Gettysburg address, or try to hear that musical selection you are trying to learn. There is nothing new about trying to see or hear something in one's imagination (you have done it many times), but it may be new to you to try to employ imagery in your learning as a type of recitation. Try it!

Sometimes we shun audible oral recitation because we think we appear foolish when "talking to ourselves," especially when someone catches us at it. We have associated talking to oneself with mental peculiarity, and the last thing we desire is to be considered mentally peculiar—even though at times we may be. Hence, we tend to avoid using recitation. If reciting aloud to yourself seems awkward, find an audience and there will be nothing peculiar about reciting orally. You can recite in the presence of others by asking them to listen to you and to check your errors. If you do the same for them, you will not be indebted to them. *Tell it to someone* and you will be using recitation.

There are other socially acceptable ways with which you are familiar in which one can recite, and which are not generally regarded as recitation. *Explain it to someone*. Perhaps there is a complex theory that you are trying to learn—explain it to someone. There may be a proof in geometry, or a law in physics that you are trying to master—explain it to someone. Every teacher will tell you that he learned more about his subject after attempting to teach it (to explain it) to others than he did before beginning to teach. Therefore, explain what you are learning to someone and learn to know it better. If two of you are learning the same thing, take turns in explaining it to each other, section by section. To gain most, each of you should explain the same things to the other (sometimes more than once) with the listener each time checking for errors.

Sometimes a somewhat less formal type of recitation than explaining can be used, namely, *discussion*. *Talk it over*. When using the discussion procedure of recitation, keep the group small (two or three is best) and if possible include someone in the discussion group who knows more about the subject than you do. A discussion can be a fruitless compounding of ignorance when no one knows anything, or at best very little, about the subject discussed. Often, things come out of a discussion that are overlooked otherwise. Discussion is a case of telling another or others what you know about a subject, and *as the result of telling, you will know it better.*

## Recitation and Other Learning Techniques

Recitation is closely related to some of the other learning techniques already discussed in Chapter 4. Let us see just how it is related to them.

*Put it into words.* Verbalize when you recite. This, we have noted, always pays dividends when learning. We have just noted above that telling someone what one has learned, or explaining it, or just discussing it will help to fix it in our memory. Each time we do one of these things we are putting our learning into words. Try it! Use some type of verbal response when you recite.

*Put it into action.* We have already noted the value of writing things out or of drawing them. This is making use of motor responses when learning. Recite by *doing something* that is active. *Do something* with what you are learning.

*Use several senses.* Although much of your studying may be reading, which is visual, recite by using several senses. Hear it, and act on it, as well as see it. These different sensations supplement each other, thus making a richer experience, and a richer and more varied experience is much more apt to stay with you for a longer time.

## OVERLEARN

### What Is Overlearning?

Overlearning is all too frequently confused with over-working and, hence, is regarded as detrimental and as something to be avoided. Overlearning, we must hasten to point out, is definitely *not* detrimental; on the contrary, it is very

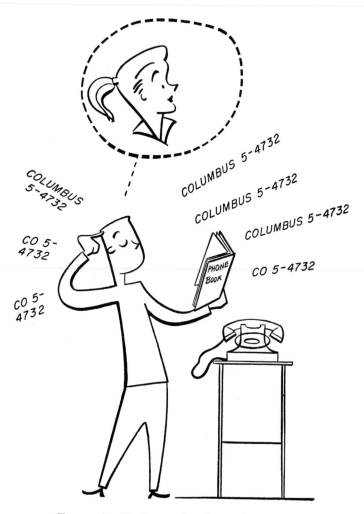

FIGURE 28. To Remember Long, Overlearn.

beneficial. Just what is overlearning? Overlearning may be defined as *that learning that one does beyond what is necessary for immediate recall.*

When you look up a telephone number in the directory, generally you repeat it only once, or possibly twice, because you intend to remember it only long enough to dial the number. If unexpectedly you get the "busy signal" and have to dial again a few minutes later, you often find that you have forgotten the number during those few minutes between calls and have to find it in the directory again. Your forgetting is due chiefly to two things: (1) you did not intend to remember the number for long; and (2) you certainly did not overlearn it.

Overlearning is that *added time and effort* beyond what is needed now that you put into learning what you intend to recall at some time in the future. A few additional repetitions *now* of that telephone number along with one or two conscious associations or observations as to the pattern of the number generally fixes it in your memory so that you remember it for a longer time—sometimes for a very long time.

Overlearning also means that one spends added time and energy learning something which one already knows. This seems to be a foolish waste of valuable time and energy that can be spent with more profit learning something else. For this reason, many students, intending to be efficient, avoid overlearning. This is a mistaken idea, if that which we are learning is to have some permanence. Of course, there is no point in overlearning everything, such as a telephone number we shall dial once and never again, nor is there any point in overlearning a grocery list that is good only today, nor the six tasks that must be completed in the next 30 minutes. We do not want or need to learn such things so thoroughly that we shall know them months or even years hence. But in the case of those things that we do intend to remember next week, or at the end of the semester, or several years hence, they must be overlearned because it is overlearning that insures longer retention. Foolish as overlearning may seem at the time (because one already knows), it does pay to overlearn because of the gain in retention. Therefore, overlearn and remember longer.

## How Much Does One Gain?

The added gain in retention is roughly proportional to the time and energy spent in overlearning. This does not mean that when you spend ten minutes rather than five minutes in overlearning that you will know twice as much or remember twice again as long. In all probability, you will remember more and longer as a result of added overlearning, but there is no rule of thumb that you can use to calculate the gain. Although added time spent overlearning does give a greater return, an excessive amount of time spent on overlearning gives diminishing returns. We need not be concerned about this here, for you are not likely to spend 400 or 500 minutes overlearning something that 12 or 20 minutes of overlearning is likely to make relatively permanent.

One final caution: *overlearning* to be effective, *must be active learning*. One's attention must be on what is being overlearned. Added time spent in vague repetition of what has just been learned will not fixate the learning. Overlearning is not a ritual with magic results that works just because one does it; it is a continuation of what has just been done. Therefore, overlearn! Overlearn actively and with conscious attention by using the several methods of recitation discussed above.

## READ EFFECTIVELY

### Poor Reading Habits

In spite of the emphasis in the last two decades on scientific research in remedial reading and improvements in the teaching of reading in the classroom, many people are inefficient readers and, hence, learn less from their reading than they can and should. Reading disabilities are of various sorts: slowness, poor comprehension, verbalization, and reading words instead of ideas. They are due to various things: eye defects, diseases, poor habits, and even hand dominance. For a fuller discussion of these aspects of poor reading and their relationship to learning, consult any of the standard works on remedial reading. For our present purpose, we are interested in two very common and especially detrimental habits that interfere with effective learning.

*Automatic reading.* You have been reading for the past 12 or more years, depending on your age. From your present point of view, it certainly seems as though you have been reading during your whole life. For the past several years, you have been reading daily and sometimes for long hours. You are no stranger to reading. Quite naturally, anything that is done as long and as often as reading tends to become rather automatic. When an activity becomes automatic, it requires less and less attention, thus freeing us to attend to other things. As far as many things are concerned, this is a fine thing. But when reading becomes automatic and fails to command conscious attention, it is unfortunate. When reading does become automatic (in this sense), we go through the motions of reading by making eye movements and turning pages without being aware, or only very vaguely aware, of what we are reading. However, having made the eye movements and having turned all the pages assigned, we too often are satisfied that we have read the assignment. True, we know little or nothing of what we have read, but we can look a teacher in the eye and say honestly, "I have read the assignment." This affirmation seems somehow to discharge the obligation of knowing the contents of the assignment.

Needless to say, such automatic reading does nothing to further one in the direction of learning. Anyone who believes that such automatic reading accomplishes something is rationalizing. The next time you observe yourself reading automatically and without conscious attention, admit that you are wasting time. Get back on the beam, and reread with conscious attention what you read automatically. Avoid automatic reading by establishing the habit of *reading ideas rather than words.*

*Reading as a ritual.* Judging by the way some students read an assignment, their reading is not only automatic but ritualistic as well. Since teachers often stress the need for reading an assignment more than once (two, three, and even more times), there are students who make a practice of reading each assignment three times. On first thought, this appears to be very commendable because it does indicate the student's willingness to spend considerable time in attempting to master an assignment. If, however, the student's technique has degenerated into a blind faith that somehow three readings of an assignment always lead to success, then his approach must be questioned. If his faith is in the magic of three readings, his reading is more than likely automatic. Why attend when the magic three readings do the trick?

The I-always-read-it-three-times student is apt to reason somewhat as follows when using this approach to studying: Since he *always* reads the material three times, he reasons that during the first time through he can afford to be inattentive, for what he misses (which may be nearly everything) during the first reading he surely will understand after the second reading. Consequently, he loafs through the assigned material, daydreaming as he turns the pages, confident that in the next two readings he will be alert and attentive. During the second reading, because his leisurely approach and inattention are habitual, he rereads the assigned material in the same ineffective way that he did the first time. Still not knowing much about that which he has read, his faith in the magic third reading is intensified. His third reading is a repetition of the first two. The habit cannot be broken. This the student frequently realizes and hence he rationalizes: "I always read an assignment three times. I have read this one three times. I still don't know what it is all about; but if a person can't get it in *three* readings, it just can't be understandable." Therefore, the student feels secure in his distorted judgment. He did read the material three times!

## Have a Plan and a Purpose

Most students need to read an assignment more than once. This is particularly true of all except those who are exceptionally gifted, and it is generally true of all when the material studied is complex and difficult. The fact is everyone, regardless of ability, profits from several readings of an assignment.

The secret of successful learning is never in the *number* of readings but in the *purpose* behind the several readings. The trouble with the student whose reading is ritualistic is that each time he reads, he reads in the same way. Instead of having a strong intention to learn something from the present reading, he hopes that he will learn something from the next reading. Instead of learning something in the present, he expects to learn something in the future. It is his attitude that is wrong.

Have a plan and a purpose. *Resolve to accomplish something definite each time you read.* Also resolve to accomplish something *different* during each reading. Have a different method of accomplishing your goal each time. Having a different purpose and a different technique for each reading will increase your attentiveness and your insistence on learning something during each reading. Substitute learning in the present for hope in future learning. Remember that learning is always accomplished in the present.

It is true that one's reading technique must be varied from time to time, depending on the ease or difficulty of the material read, one's insight into it, and one's familiarity with it. A general plan, however, that is effective much of the time and that does give excellent results is outlined below.

*Reconnaissance reading.*   One's purpose during the first reading of an assignment should be to get a *general acquaintance* with what is presented. During the first reading of an assignment, one should learn the broad organization of the material assigned, the major topics covered, the author's plan of development, and the general conclusion to which the discussion leads. As a result of this first reading, one's view should be a broad, overall view. Therefore, we shall call this type of reading reconnaissance reading.

One's reading technique when doing reconnaissance reading should be to read rapidly. If you do not understand some parts as you read them, continue reading. It may be that the points you do not understand will be cleared up as you read further, and if they are not, you can always return to them at a later time. Remember your purpose in this first reading: to gain a *broad view* of what is covered. Hurry on in your reading, for in this way you will grasp the broader aspects of the subject most quickly.

To stop studying an assignment after your first or recon-

RECONNAISSANCE
READING
FLY THROUGH

ANALYTICAL
READING
WORK THROUGH

TERMINAL
READING
HURRY THROUGH

FIGURE 29. Three Types of Reading.

naissance reading can be fatal as far as ultimate mastery of the subject is concerned. Reconnaissance reading is only the beginning. Of course, there are students who say: "All I want is a general view of the subject, so why reread it?" The student who is satisfied with stopping after a reconnaissance reading of an assignment fails to appreciate that what he thinks is a general view may turn out to be a hazy view. General ideas and broad views of a subject come only as the result of knowing details; thus, one must proceed to the second type of reading, namely, analytical reading.

*Analytical reading.* The purpose of analytical reading, in contrast to reconnaissance reading, is to *discover the details,* the specific results, the facts out of which the general ideas and the broader view of the subject are developed. Analytical reading means doing spade work—digging out the facts and observations on which the thinking rests. The purpose of analytical reading, then, is to learn the details.

Just as the purpose of analytical reading differs from reconnaissance reading, so its technique differs also. Analytical reading requires one to read more slowly, to reread sentences and paragraphs that are not understood clearly. When using the analytical approach, tables and graphs are examined with care and the implications in the data presented are noted. Moreover, in analytical reading one returns to material already read in order to tie it in with what is now being read.

Progress during analytical reading is slow compared with reconnaissance reading; this reading will require more time than any of the others. It is the reading in which one's major learning is done. It is the reading in which details become alive and meaningful because they are related to the general pattern of the material discovered in the initial reconnaissance reading.

One final and important instruction with regard to technique when using analytical reading is: use a pencil. This will be discussed fully in the next major section of this chapter.

*Terminal reading.* One can stop studying after using analytical reading, but it is advisable to complete one's work on an assignment by using what we here call terminal reading.

The purpose of terminal reading is to bring together the many details, facts, and observations noted so carefully in one's second or analytical reading, and to see them in broad perspective and in relationship to the whole. Terminal reading integrates the material into an understandable whole. In terminal reading, one again reads rapidly, skipping through the text, noting particularly those things which were marked during one's analytical reading. Perhaps the best time to do terminal reading is just prior to a class period or a test. Terminal reading refreshes one's memory and provides perspective.

## Space Your Reading

The study-rest-study-rest method of learning, presented in Chapter 4, is one of the most effective methods of learning. Take advantage of it when your assignments involve a great deal of reading. Incorporate this method into your reading procedure. More specifically, after completing your reconnaissance reading of an assignment, turn to something else that is different—have a rest pause. Later that day, or perhaps the next, return to the material that you are broadly familiar with and reread it analytically. Mark your text; dig it out. After this major attack on the assignment, put it aside again and return to it to do your terminal reading just before going to class or to a test. This terminal reading, which may take only fifteen or twenty minutes, will refresh your memory and prepare you finally for the day's recitation or test.

Remember that all three of these types of reading are parts of a plan of study. Therefore, do not rely on just one of them, and certainly not on only the first and the last because they happen to be the ones that take less time. When your time available for study is relatively short, the type of reading that you need most is the second type—analytical reading.

## MARK YOUR BOOK

### Textbooks Are Expendable

A textbook is a tool to be used, a tool for learning. Textbooks, like other tools, are expensive. Also, not a few of them are attractive in appearance, just as many modern tools are styled to appeal to one's aesthetic sense. Because they are expensive and attractive in appearance does not mean that they must be guarded like antique treasures. Neither should they be placed in a dust-proof case and exhibited like the trophies of a safari. Textbooks are made to be used. *They are expendable.*

I have known students who were reluctant to open a new textbook lest the binding be broken. Some students place no marks in their texts because of a childish awe of books and the fear that any mark will desecrate the book. Some students impractically do not even write their name in their book, so strong is the notion that a book must be cherished like a jewel.

From whence comes this almost reverent attitude toward books? True, it is a part of our culture to hold books in high regard. This attitude probably stems from the period of our pioneer days when the Bible was the only book, or very nearly the only book, in the home. As other books were added to the book shelf, they too were highly regarded. Books generally continue to be regarded highly and therefore must not be misused, and marking them amounts to misuse. Moreover, children from an early age are admonished to resist the temptation to mark in books. This training is desirable and necessary, for many of the books a child sees these days are library books that must not be scribbled in. Besides, indiscriminate scribbling in a book certainly adds nothing to its value. The point is, the lesson of not scribbling in books is learned so thoroughly by children, and they are so strongly conditioned emotionally against it, that at a later time many of them cannot allow themselves to mark in a textbook even though they should do so intelligently and with purpose.

A mechanic or a craftsman buys a tool to use it. A carpenter buys a saw to saw boards with, not to display it on his mantel or to show it off to his friends when they call at his home. He buys it to use it. Since use dulls a saw, the carpenter must sharpen it almost daily by filing it. Naturally, filing wears it away until finally the carpenter must discard it and buy a new one.

A textbook, like the carpenter's saw, is also a tool—*a tool that is used in the business of learning.* As in the case of other tools, *a textbook must be used* if one expects to get a maximum return on one's investment in it. As a result of intensive use, the textbook (the tool used in learning) like other tools may be worn out. Don't let this alarm you; that is why you bought it. Remember, the purpose of a textbook is use. Use it!

## Why Some Students Save Textbooks

Students are motivated variously to save and protect their textbooks. Some are textbook collectors. Not that they will ever need or use them in the future; they are just collectors. Then there are those who just "like books." There are those who believe that a once-used textbook is tangible proof of their knowledge of a subject, and they must always have this tangible proof available to convince doubters and sceptics. There are also those people who believe that what *they* have studied is the ultimate in knowledge and therefore will continue to be true for all time, and they must have their old textbooks to prove it. Finally, some students save textbooks so that they will have something to fill that mantel book shelf that they hope will be in their dream home ten years after graduation.

True, some books are worth saving, and some are even worth saving for a long time, but is your chief purpose in buying a textbook to save it for a future and indefinite purpose, or to use it now—*today*—to learn something that is of value to you now and in all probability will be of value to you in the future? If your purpose in purchasing a textbook is to use it now, as I am sure that it is, then use it!

### Make the Material Your Own

Reading that which another has written often leaves the reader with the feeling that the ideas are the author's possession. Evidence of this is found in class recitations when students say, "They say," when referring to the text, rather than saying, "I think . . . or I believe . . . or I know . . ." To learn, one must make the material his own. He must *personalize* it. How can one personalize the material in a textbook?

Make the textbook your own by putting yourself into it. Put *your stamp* on it. This can be done by marking the book. Do not use just any marks, but marks that show discrimination, organization, evaluation, insight, relationships, associations, and new ideas. Use marks that are meaningful to you and that help you to grasp the significance of what the author is attempting to say to you. *Mark your book generously, but with discrimination.* Use a pencil rather than a pen [5] so that you can change your notations as you gain insight into the author's thinking.

Use different types of notations that are meaningful to you to indicate different things. There are no particular rules about this, but here are a few suggestions. Very important things can be underscored. If underscoring is reserved for major points, it should be used sparingly. I once saw a history book in which a student underscored in ink *every line* on *every page* in a *whole chapter.* What a waste of time, energy, and ink. All the student needed to do in this case was to write the words "very important" on the first page of the chapter. Not only was his underscoring senseless; it was also very messy and slowed down his reading.

A vertical line drawn in the margin calls attention to an important sentence or short paragraph. Somewhat greater importance can be indicated by drawing two parallel vertical lines in the margin, or by substituting a wavy line for the straight line.

Underscoring important *words,* rather than whole sentences, often brings out ideas that seem to be buried among phrases and subordinate clauses. Even encircling words or phrases that are somewhat remote from each other, and grouping them together by drawing light lines from the one word or phrase to the other (right across the intervening print) is a useful technique.

Numbering points made in a paragraph or section of a textbook not only indicates the number of points made, but emphasizes their importance. Other useful marginal notes

[5] Ink is not only permanent, but often penetrates the paper to such an extent that it is seen on the next page. This makes for confusion, for the marks showing on the next page may be taken as marking something on that page which they are not intended to mark.

cultivating family pride, and protecting the family name. Responsibility in the home is not encouraged, and group recreation in the family is the exception. Because the delinquent learns that he has little in common with his parents, and that they have little or no interest in him, he turns elsewhere—outside the home—in his quest for affection, entertainment, and security.

### Activities Outside of the Home

The activities of delinquents outside of the home seem to indicate a desire to achieve three things: (1) to escape from restraint; (2) to experience adventure; and (3) to find oblivion in the group.

1. The desire to escape from restraint and regulation is evident in delinquents' dislike for organized recreation, poor adjustment to school routine, frequent truancy, lack of interest in competitive activities, and irregularity in church attendance. Even in their employment they tend to enter the street trades where supervision is less. This dislike of routine, rules of action, and domination by adults, may stem from the excessively dominant or *laissez faire* attitudes of the home.

2. Delinquents' desire for excitement and adventure stands out prominently in their leisure-time activities. They do things and
   a. go places where the risk is great. They hop trucks, steal rides, sneak into movies, frequent the waterfront and the railroad yards, stay out late nights, and roam the streets after dark. They run away from home, "bunk out" nights, set fires, destroy property,
   b. and indulge in petty stealing. They are precocious in smoking, in drinking, and in having sexual experiences. About a half of them
   c. attend the movies excessively. Even in their employment they enter the various street trades where the chances for excitement are definitely greater.

   This craving for adventure probably also stems from the home —the home that is dull, uninteresting, emotionally cold, and full of conflict. In contrast to the home, the delinquent's outside activities offer excitement and adventure—release from tensions and pent-up emotions.

3. The third characteristic of delinquents is their desire for group membership. They gang together. Younger boys seek the com-

FIGURE 30. Illustration Showing How a Textbook Can Be Marked to Make the Material One's Own. (From G. J. Dudycha, *Psychology for Law Enforcement Officers,* Springfield, Illinois, Charles C. Thomas, 1955, p. 264. Reproduced with the permission of the publisher.)

panionship of older boys probably because of identification and
the feeling of greater security. They also participate in delinquent
acts with others because of the anonymity that the gang offers.
Numbers also give a sense of strength and invincibility. Hence the
gang satisfies fundamental desires, and gives a feeling of belonging,
not found in the home.

## THE PSYCHOLOGY OF FRUSTRATION

### The Importance of Motivation

To understand the behavior of people one must have insight
into that which motivates them. By motivation we do not mean
that which the layman has in mind when he uses the word "motive."
A motive, in this sense, is a reason for action. Sometimes it is
scarcely more than a verbalization. Psychologically conceived,
motivation is all those factors, activities and experiences that predispose one to act in a certain way rather than in other ways.

Should a person address us in an insulting way, we may hit
him, be insulting in return, walk away quietly, or be kind to him.
What we do depends on our training, "gang" experiences, Boy
Scout background, Sunday School and religious training, past
insults, present associates, past fights or social successes, contacts
with a favorite teacher, and a host of other things. All these things
condition us—predispose us—to behave in the way we do behave
at the moment.

Although much of this predisposition to behave in particular
ways is *individual*, there are some broad similarities that we find
in most people. W. I. Thomas[2] has stressed four such broad motivating factors that he calls desires. These are the desires for new
experience, for security, for response, and for recognition. True
these four desires may not exhaust the list, but all are fundamental
and all are important to an understanding of delinquency because
the delinquent satisfies these desires in abnormal ways.

The delinquent's desire for new experience expresses itself in
his roaming the streets at night, running away from home, hopping
trucks, frequenting waterfront areas and scores of other things
that are a part of his eagerness for adventure. His desire for

---

[2]Thomas, W. I.: *The Unadjusted Girl*. Boston, Little, Brown and Company, 1923.

FIGURE 30 (*Continued*)

are the question mark, check mark, exclamation mark, the cross, and other similar marks that either have or can be given specific meanings.

Marginal notations in the form of words, phrases, and brief comments should be used frequently. References to earlier or later pages that deal with related material tie parts of the text together. Notations on your own past experiences that are related to the text, and drawings or sketches are also very useful.

By making the kinds of notations in your textbooks that we have noted above, you will put something of yourself into the book. The words and ideas will no longer be the sole property of the author; they will be your ideas as well. To do this is a psychological experience. Try it and discover that it does make a difference in your learning.

There is one final caution with regard to the application of this method of learning: *be sure that the book you mark is your own.* Do not, under any circumstances, use this method when using a library book or a book borrowed from a friend. Do not impose your personality on a book that is public property and that someone else is going to use. For the same reason, it is not well to use second-hand textbooks that other students before you have "personalized." It is very difficult to make material your own that has been "possessed" by someone else before you. Make your own interpretation of what you are studying. Put *your* stamp on it.

## SOME MINOR TECHNIQUES OF LEARNING

### Outlining

Outlining, a technique that is used very widely, has some advantages and some disadvantages. The technique, in all probability, is of sufficient familiarity to you that no lengthy discussion of its nature is necessary here. The purpose of an outline is to identify the major divisions of the material being studied, to find the subdivisions under each of these, and to identify the more detailed points subsumed under these. The outline serves to divide textual material into parts and reveals the *pattern of its organization*. Outlining is particularly easy when the author of the text followed an outline when writing, or when the material is of a very factual sort.

The advantage of the outline, then, lies in the fact that it reveals the organization and evaluation of the material. In doing so, it does facilitate learning. However, the mere making of an outline does not mean that the student has made the material his own. The outline, as well as the material, may still be the author's. This, I find, is one of the chief shortcomings of outlining as used by many students. They believe that somehow, because they have made an outline, they know the material. Too often, unfortunately, they do not know what they have outlined.

Another disadvantage of outlining is that some material is much more difficult to outline than other material. Hence, a student may wrestle with the construction of a good outline and be so intent on making a good outline, that he fails to grasp the ideas which the author seeks to convey.

Since outlining involves a great deal of writing, it can be a very time-consuming technique. Marking one's own text is much faster. When the book belongs to another person, however, or to a school or a library, outlining is sometimes an unavoidable necessity.

## Writing Abstracts

Some students like to write a brief, to-the-point summary of each major topic covered in an assignment, a summary which they use when reviewing for a test or an examination.

A student may make such an abstract in history covering the battle of Gettysburg; or in physics, of a theory; or in chemistry, of an industrial process. An abstract must always be short (seldom more than 200 or 300 words), cover all major points, and enumerate pertinent details. Students who do not like to write are not apt to employ this method of learning; but students who do like to write find it valuable, not only because it forces one to evaluate the many items involved in what one is learning, but because it forces one to do something about it—to write it out.

## Using Question-Cards

This technique is similar to that of writing abstracts, except that that which is written (the answer) is generally short and definitely related to a specific question. The answers are generally written on three-by-five or on four-by-six cards and then related questions are grouped together. The disadvantages of this method are two: the fragmentation of knowledge rather than relatedness, and the tendency toward memorization rather than insight and understanding.

# WHOLE VERSUS PART LEARNING
## The Nature of the Methods

The difference between whole and part learning is in the way the material to be learned is dealt with. As the term "whole method" implies, that which is learned is always dealt with as a whole. When one memorizes a poem by reading the entire poem through again and again until it is learned, one is using the *whole method*. Logic favors this method in that one's learning consists entirely of doing what one wants to be able to do ultimately, namely, to repeat the poem.

The *part method,* on the other hand, is a case of breaking the whole up into parts and learning the parts part by part.

Learning a poem by the part method means that one learns it line by line or stanza by stanza, not going on to the next line or stanza until the previous one has been learned. As each part is learned in its turn the whole poem is finally mastered.

A third, intermediate method, called the *progressive part method,* is used by many learners. By this method the poem is learned line by line or stanza by stanza, as in the part method, but after the first and second parts are learned the two are repeated together, thus making them into a unit. Then the third part is learned and subsequently added to the first two, and now the three are repeated. This process is continued until the whole poem is mastered.

## The Value of the Methods

Experimental data do not clearly favor any one of these methods over the others. In fact, on the basis of experimental results one may say: use whichever method you prefer. By preference the progressive part method is generally favored by most learners. The whole method is much more apt to be used by gifted learners, whose grasp of details is broad, than by the more average learners. In any case, these methods apply chiefly when one is memorizing verbatim such things as poetry, prose, lines in a play, or similar material. Use of these methods is limited and the benefits are not at all certain.

# 6.

## Learning Skills

### THE NATURE OF SKILLS

#### Skills Are Interesting

Skills fascinate people. Have you ever watched a juggler keep five teacups in the air without dropping a single one, or a knife-thrower outline the figure of a pretty girl with knives thrown from a considerable distance? If you have, your reaction to their flawless skill most likely was: "Do it again!" If your interests tend more toward the aesthetic than the spectacular, you may recall a performance of the Rockettes in New York's Radio City Music Hall. If so, you recall the perfect precision and remarkable skill demonstrated by a chorus line of 36 almost identical girls. One never tires of the beauty of their performance because of their perfect rhythm and consummate skill.

Each one of us can think of many instances when he witnessed unusual skill. I remember seeing a man born armless who wrote by holding a pen between the first and second toes of his right foot. In spite of his handicap, he wrote beautifully, and all who paid to see him agreed that this man "wrote a beautiful foot."

We are fascinated not only by the spectacular, but by the

prosaic skills as well. A person who writes exceptionally well engages our interest, especially since so many of us write so poorly. Even the power-shovel operator elicits our admiration for his skill in handling the powerful machine every time he places that clumsy-looking bucket in just the right spot, takes a big bite, and dumps its load exactly where he wants it. That his skill does fascinate people is attested to by the number of "sidewalk superintendents" on duty each time the power-shovel operator is working.

Why do you enjoy football and basketball games, tennis matches, swimming meets, and other such athletic events? To see your team win? Yes, of course, but this is not the only nor even the chief reason you are an enthusiastic sports fan. The chief reason you are an enthusiastic spectator is that you enjoy seeing skillful performance, even in a member of the opponent's team. Do you remain in the bleachers long when every play is a fumble, just because your team has fumbled less? Do you enjoy seeing an intended swan dive that turns out to be a polar-bear flop? Probably not, not even when the damsel is a model and your intended!

We like to see others perform skillfully. Even such everyday skills as walking with poise, typing accurately with speed, and shuffling a deck of cards with dexterity interests us. Moreover, we are interested in doing these things skillfully ourselves. Therefore, it is the purpose of this chapter to aid us in discovering the technique of learning these and many other everyday skills quickly, efficiently, effectively, and with less effort.

## What Is a Skill?

Skills are sometimes defined rather academically as neuromuscular coördinations that are learned. This distinguishes them from reflexes that are native. Sometimes *skill* learning

is contrasted with *knowledge* learning. This approach contrasts doing with knowing. Although this distinction has some
merit, one must not infer that any muscle twitch or series of
such twitches that involves no knowledge is a skill.

Several things are essential to our concept of skill. First, it
is an activity, generally a *muscular activity*.[1] Furthermore, it
is a *proficient* act. By this we mean that a skill is organized
activity; that it is sequential; that extraneous or unnecessary
activities are absent; and that muscular tension is at a minimum. Finally, the result of this proficient response (or that
which is produced) has quality, good form, and sometimes
approaches perfection. In fact, it is this matter of proficiency
that distinguishes the term "skill" from the term "habit"
with which it is closely associated. *A skill is a proficient habit.*

A proficient response is made automatically and with a
minimum of attention. Generally, we skip rope, unlock a
door, or brush our teeth with very little or even with no attention to the various phases of the total activity. Each step
in the cycle leads automatically to the next until the whole
cycle is completed, and in some cases is repeated many times,
as in the case of skipping rope. This automatic nature of a
skill is due to the fact that we have learned to respond to
cues, mostly kinesthetic in nature, that in each case initiate
the next activity. Kinesthetic sensations result from the movement of muscles, tendons, and joints. Since there is nothing
spectacular about these sensations as there is about visual and
auditory ones, we are wholly unaware of their presence. Yet,
they are always present whenever a muscle or muscle group
moves, and they are the cues on which we depend in every
skill. *Learning a skill is a case of learning to respond to these
kinesthetic cues* to which we do not consciously attend.

There is one final aspect that we must recognize as im-

[1] It may also be a glandular activity, as in the case of the actress who
is *skilled* in turning on and off tears when acting.

portant in skilled activity, namely, its relation to perception. A skilled act is almost never a blind act. The person performing the skilled act is not only responding to kinesthetic cues, as we have just noted, but he is also responding to visual, auditory, tactual, and other sensory cues that are meaningful to him. A skilled automobile driver does not go through a cycle of activity blindly when driving; on the contrary, he sets in motion a sequence of activity (a skill) according to the way he perceives road conditions—traffic flowing in the opposite direction, road hazards, highway signs at the side of the road, and so on. If a skilled motorist *perceives* a traffic signal flash red 100 yards down the road, he *knows* that this means stop or danger ahead, and hence he moves his foot at the right time from the accelerator to the brake pedal which he depresses the right amount in order to stop the car just as it reaches the traffic signal. This sequence of activity (deceleration and braking) is the skill that is set going by the driver's *perception of the situation* and his *knowledge* of the speed with which he is traveling, the effectiveness of his brakes, how well his tires grip the roadway, and the like.

Thus, we must conclude that skill has its perceptual (meaning) and its cognitive (knowing) aspects as well as its motor aspect. Therefore, to learn skills one must relate motor sequences to perceptual or meaningful experiences, sensory cues, and knowledge.

## ATTITUDE TOWARD LEARNING SKILLS

Every skill is intended to accomplish something; each has a purpose. This purpose may be to entertain (as in juggling), to communicate (as in writing), to build a table (as in cabinet-making), or to get a ball over the goal line (as in football). Because most of the things accomplished by skills are important and some produce tangible results, much emphasis is generally placed on what is accomplished or on the end result. When people seek to learn a skill they are prone to think in terms of that which is *accomplished or produced*. The person who wants to write legibly sees "in his mind's eye" a specimen of excellent handwriting; the person who wants to learn to typewrite sees a perfectly typed manuscript. The learner all too often assumes that his task in learning a skill is to duplicate, by some vaguely understood means, the specimen he has in mind or observes. There is much more to learning skills than this.

It has been said often that there is a right way of doing everything. When this right way is achieved, we consider that the skill is developed nearly to its maximum. To learn any skill, primary emphasis must be placed on the *process* by which the goal or end result is achieved rather than on what is accomplished or produced.

We must admit, however, that emphasis on or attention to the goal does at times result in learning to produce that goal. Left-handed children do learn to write, under the usually ineffective tutelage of right-handed teachers, by attempting to reproduce in their own way the specimen that is before them. One need merely observe the many very awkward and inefficient ways in which most left-handed students write to be convinced that this method of learning a skill is very unsatisfactory.

One can also learn to play golf by concentrating on the goal of rolling the ball into the cup, but every serious golfer knows that concentration on stance, grip, back-swing, down-swing, and follow-through inevitably results in better golf scores.

It is true that to learn any skill one must be familiar with the goal or that which is to be accomplished, but *learning*

FIGURE 31. Learn to Play Golf by Watching the Golfer
Rather than the Ball.

*the skill* that results in such accomplishment *consists of establishing a sequence of activities* that are cued by kinesthetic sensations and that are oriented to the situation or environment in which one must perform that skill.

Therefore, when learning a new skill, note consciously what specific responses are made; note the order in which they are made; become familiar with the "feel" of each movement, and relate all this to the environmental stimuli that are important to this skill. *Learn with intention!*

## PROGRESS MADE IN LEARNING SKILLS

### The Intention to Learn

In the foregoing section we emphasized *learning with intention.* The intention to learn is primary for all goal-oriented learning. Since skills are goal-oriented, the intention to learn is primary for them also. Although incidental learning (learning without intention) does occur, we can hardly rely on that type of learning in the school situation or in the workaday world where things must get done and a high level of achievement is generally demanded. Therefore, the first essential for the learning of skills is to *want to learn.*

Improvement in a skill also comes only with the *intention to improve.* Some men play golf for years with no greater skill now than they had ten or twenty years ago. The reason for their lack of improvement is that they play the game for the exercise or for the social contacts it affords with little desire to improve their scores.

Do you have a strong desire to improve your skills? Take the matter of handwriting, for example. You have been writing script for more than a decade now, and with what results! Do your teachers commend you on the excellence of your handwriting? Would you get the blue ribbon in a writing contest? Or is it true of you that after practicing handwriting most of your life, even you have difficulty reading it? If so, why? The reason is that you, like many people, have little intention to improve this skill. To improve a skill, one must *want to improve it!*

### Early Stages of Learning

Recall your first attempts to swim or to play tennis. Your first conception of the former was to be able to get from one side of the pool to the other by a series of vigorous, but seemingly random, slashing movements of arms and legs; your conception of the latter was to bat the ball over the net by running to the right spot in the court and contacting the ball with the racket. Your intention in each of these skills was to *accomplish something* (get to the other side of the pool or to put the ball over the net) by some means vaguely understood.

You have come a long way from these first attempts, if you are a good swimmer or an expert tennis player now. How did you come to your present stage of expertness? One thing is quite certain: you developed each of these skills gradually by noting the parts of the total act of swimming and of tennis playing. Little by little, you became aware that the vague slashing of arms and legs had to give way to a particular stroke. The stroke itself, you found, was complicated, for you had to learn to do certain things with each hand and with each arm, and not at just any time but at the right time. Hand and arm movements had to be coördinated with leg movements which were also complicated. All of these activities had to be coördinated with trunk movements and with breathing. In learning to play tennis, you went through a corresponding series of stages. In general, your progress in learning these skills was from a vague conception of the total activity to acquaintance with many specific activities that had to be patterned and coördinated. You went from the whole activity to many partial activities which you gradually integrated into the whole activity.

When beginning to learn a new skill, do not be distressed by the fact that it strikes you as a vague jumble of many activities, which is the usual reaction. When this is true, you are still seeing the activity as a whole. After you begin to break the activity down into its parts and perceive the parts or details as such and in relationship to each other, the total aspect of the skill will begin to appear more simple and comprehensible.

Therefore, to facilitate learning when mastering a new skill, one should first attempt to duplicate the whole activity a number of times in order to get the general idea of the whole response. This should be followed as quickly as possible by an examination of the part activities and the ways in which they are patterned. When this is done, the total activity begins to take on new meaning and its complexity appears to decrease. The result: the learner is encouraged and his intention to learn is strengthened. As this cycle continues to be repeated, the learner progresses toward greater mastery of the new skill.

**Progress Toward Skillful Performance**

*The whole body is involved.* Try to learn the skill of wiggling your ears. This skill is of questionable value, but it will serve our purpose. If you are not now an ear-wiggler, you will find great difficulty in discovering the muscles that move your ears. If you are intent to learn, however, you will find yourself doing many things in the beginning, most of which have nothing to do with wiggling your ears. Try it! In all probability, you are finding that you are moving your scalp, making faces, wrinkling your nose, setting your jaw, tensing neck muscles, moving one or both shoulders, clenching your fists, crossing and recrossing your legs, squirming in your chair, and possibly other things. Although you are trying only to wiggle your ears, you are actually wiggling your whole body.

A child learning to write does much the same things. He not only grasps the pencil much too firmly, he also presses down on the desk with his other hand, bites his tongue or lip, squints his eyes, moves his head frequently, hooks his toes around the legs of the chair, and does many other things all of which have no part in handwriting.

This is characteristic when learning skills. One is *entirely* involved in learning the skill, which means that he makes responses that are detrimental as well as useless in the beginning. Gradually these useless responses are eliminated and only the useful ones retained and firmly fixed. To facilitate the learning of a skill, one must not only pick out the essential responses and try to fix them firmly, but he must also note the useless responses that he is making and try to eliminate them as rapidly as possible. This elimination of the extraneous responses that are so large a part of anyone's early attempts to establish a skill is often slow and difficult, but by giving attention to it, progress toward a high level of efficiency is hastened.

*The variability of response is decreased.* In the early stages of learning any skill, there is much variability of response. In basketball, dart throwing, or rifle practice one often overshoots or undershoots his mark. Sometimes one hits the bull's-eye squarely; at other times one misses the target entirely. This variability is reduced by attending to the kinesthetic and other sensory cues when one achieves the right coördination. To reduce variability, then, *concentrate on what you do when you succeed.* Intend to reduce variability and you in all probability will do so.

*Conscious attention is decreased.* One of the advantages

of learning a skill is that it enables one to perform an act or series of acts with a minimum of thinking or conscious attention. If, after several years of driving an automobile, you still had to concentrate on the details of acceleration, braking, shifting, and steering, you would find "going for a ride" with an attractive companion a chore rather than a joy. Thus, skills enable us to do more than one thing at the same time.

The need for conscious attention decreases when the essential sensory cues become so effectively related to specific acts of the skill that the various acts follow the cues automatically. To achieve this stage of the skill as early as possible, concentrate on establishing the cue-response sequences as rapidly as possible.

*Changes in perception are made.* As one establishes the initial phases of a skill, the responses made and the objects and materials used come to be perceived in new and different ways. These new ways of "seeing" one's task and that with which one works open new opportunities for advancement in the development of the skill. It is this "oh-I-see-now" experience that you have had so many times.

To speed the learning of a skill, try deliberately to perceive the elements of the situation in new ways. The more varied your perception, the more rapid your learning is likely to be.

## The Habit Hierarchy

More than half a century ago Bryan and Harter,[1] who studied the skills of sending and receiving telegraphic code, discovered the essential nature of the progress made in learning these and related skills. They found that after students learned the combination of dots and dashes for each of the

[1] W. L. Bryan and N. Harter, Studies in the physiology and psychology of telegraphic language, *Psychological Review*, 1897, 4: 27–53.

letters of the alphabet, which they called "letter habits," continued practice in sending messages resulted not only in an increased speed in sending and receiving as such, but that something new emerged which they called "word habits." At this stage of their learning, the senders did not just tap out the dots and dashes for the letters, as "o," "u," and "t," separately; instead they tapped out all the dots and dashes for the whole word "o-u-t" as a single unit. Still further practice, they found, resulted in students sending a whole phrase, as "o-u-t o-f o-r-d-e-r," as a single unit or whole. These higher-order units Bryan and Harter called "phrase habits." Book,[2] several years later, reported essentially the same results concerning the learning of typewriting.

We must not conclude that because these researchers found three levels of habits (letter, word, and phrase habits) that the same is true of every skill. The reason for the three levels of learning in sending telegraphic code and in typewriting is that both involve language. Skills of varied complexity not involving language may have fewer or more such levels of habit patterns.

Let us take your car-driving skill as a convenient illustration. When you began receiving driving instruction, there seemed to be so many things to learn that you may have despaired of ever learning to drive. First, you inserted the key into the lock; then you activated the starter; and as the motor started, you depressed the accelerator. Each of these things was a separate thing that had to be done. If you learned on a car with a standard shift, you had to learn to depress the clutch, to shift into low gear, to release the clutch and to accelerate simultaneously. Each of these things stood out as separate from the others. Then you repeated this last

[2] W. F. Book, *The Psychology of Skill,* Missoula, Montana Press, 1908.

cycle twice more in intermediate and in high gear before you really got under way, which meant that many more things had to be done. If you will count them, you will find that you had to do something like 15 things before you got the car rolling in high gear. *Fifteen things!* No wonder you were appalled at the number of things you had to learn. And this was not all, for you still had to learn to steer, to brake, to back, and to park.

Now, as you reflect on your driving skill, you think of it as a relatively simple skill. How did it become so? The answer is: by establishing simple habits first; then later by integrating a number of these into a larger unit; and later still by integrating several of these larger units into still larger wholes.

In the beginning, each act required its own habit. Inserting the key into the lock was one; turning the key in a given direction was the second, separate habit. Likewise, depressing the clutch, controlling the accelerator, and operating the shifting lever required separate habits. After a time, however, inserting the key into the lock in a particular way and activating the starter came to be one continuous response which you now execute with a minimum of conscious attention. The clutch, accelerator, and shifting responses, too, gradually came to be integrated into a single, continuous response. The transfer of learning then facilitated the establishment of the related cycles of shifting into intermediate and into high gear. Now that you are an experienced driver, you go through all these many habits in a continuous, uninterrupted way and without hesitation because all of these "second-order" habits are now integrated into still more complex and comprehensive habit patterns.

In the past, you have established many such hierarchies of habits, and as you go through college you will establish many more. There are the complex habit patterns that you will establish in athletic sports, such as, in basketball, badminton, tennis, tumbling, and perhaps fly-casting. If you enter the field of business, you may establish the skills of operating complex bookkeeping machines, calculators, and other such equipment. In art, you will learn the skills of painting and sculpturing; in music, you may learn to play the organ, harp, piano, or some other instrument. There are also the complex skills that you may learn in engineering, in science, in dentistry, in medicine, and in many other occupations and professions.

**Overlearning Skills**

It is common to overlearn skills. By overlearning we mean learning the skill so well, by a great deal of practice, that even though the skill is not used for a long time, the person still retains a marked degree of proficiency. Riding a bicycle, ice- and roller-skating are skills that people generally overlearn to such a degree that even though they do not do these things for many years, they still retain a rather large measure of their former proficiency. Overlearning, then, is learning beyond the point of minimal proficiency by repeated exercise of the skill.

Overlearning makes for long retention, and therefore it should always be kept in mind when learning a skill. If the skill is worth establishing in the first place, it is probably worth establishing so well that it will be retained for some time, perhaps for a very long time. *Overlearn* skills; *make them a permanent part of you.*

**Limits of Learning**

There are two limits of skilled learning: the practical limit and the physiological limit.

*The practical limit.*   When a person achieves a proficiency that satisfies him, that enables him to compete reasonably successfully with others, and beyond which he rarely if ever achieves, then he is in all probability operating at his practical limit. A person may learn to typewrite at the easy rate of 45 words per minute. If this rate satisfies his employer, and is about the same rate as that used by other people in his office, then this person may never feel the need for increasing his rate beyond his usual 45 words per minute. This rate becomes his practical limit. Many people operate at their practical limit in such skills as handwriting, playing a musical instrument, operating business machines, dancing, and playing golf. The practical limit generally represents a person's comfortable rate or way of performing a skill. To progress in your learning, *do not be satisfied with a low practical limit of performance.*

*The physiological limit.*   This limit of learning is one's maximum level of performance or one's highest possible achievement. One's physiological limit is approached gradually and only as a result of much practice and overlearning. Most people never achieve their physiological limit in any of the skills they learn. Moreover, if one's physiological limit is attained in any skill, generally it is not maintained for long. In spite of these observations, if one wants to compete successfully and with distinction with those people he must compete against, he should strive continually to approach his maximum limit of learning.

*Factors affecting the limits of learning.*   Some of the factors that affect one's limit of learning cannot be altered or improved. One cannot change the nature of his nervous system or his body proportions, both of which affect the learning of certain skills. The physical equipment that one must work with also affects one's proficiency. Most typists can type more words per minute on an electric typewriter than on a standard one. Working conditions (temperature, humidity, noise, and so forth) are also factors in proficiency. Some of these conditions can be changed and improved; others cannot.

There are some things, however, that you can do something about. One of these is your *method of learning* the skill. Are you satisfied to learn by following a hit-and-miss method, or are you taking advantage of that which is known to pay dividends in skilled learning? The effective methods that you can use are presented in the next section of this chapter. Become thoroughly familiar with them! Learn to apply them! Don't fail to use them each time you are learning a new skill or improving an old one.

A second thing that you can do is to set for yourself an *aspiration level* that is commensurate with your assets and possibilities. Don't be satisfied with mediocrity when you can attain to high achievement. Beware, however, of setting for yourself an impossible goal (as a bid for social prestige) that means inevitable failure. Examine your capabilities carefully; set your goal accordingly.

The third thing you can do is to *work with vigor and determination*. Avoid half-hearted learning! If the skill is worth learning at all, it is worth learning well. Learn with intention! Be an enthusiastic learner!

## AIDS AND TECHNIQUES

### Emphasize Good Form

That there is a right way of doing anything is trite but true. Therefore, study the *technique* by means of which a certain thing is accomplished, for it is always the technique that accounts for *superior* accomplishment.

You may be fascinated by the way a baseball curves in its

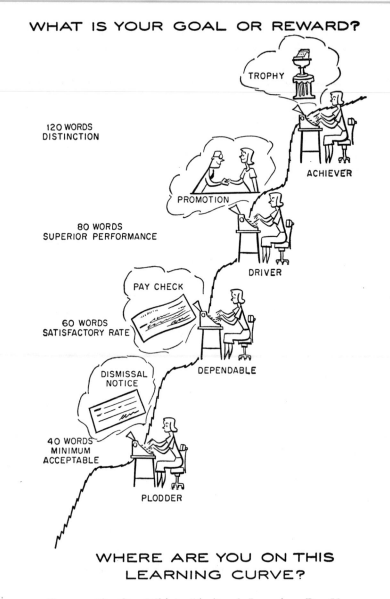

FIGURE 32. On Which Limit of Learning Do You Operate?

flight from the pitcher to the catcher. If you want to throw a curved ball, you must concentrate on the pitcher and on what he does much more than on the curved ball. You must discover how he holds the ball; how he controls each arm and the wrist of his throwing hand; the movements he makes with his trunk and legs; and his timing as well as the sequence of his movements. Analyze his movements carefully; *pattern your actions* after what you perceive him do. Then, when you ultimately duplicate his complex, well-coördinated response, the balls you will throw will curve as his do.

When learning a skill, always stress performance much more than the end result if you desire to achieve to a high level of skill. Emphasis on the end result, and only on the end result, ends in mediocrity.

One day a novice and an expert golfer were playing a round of golf. The novice knew enough about the game to know that the ball has to be hit with a club and that the object of the game is to drive the ball to the next green and to drop it into the cup with the fewest strokes possible. He knew what was to be accomplished (the end result) for he had seen what others accomplish; what he did not know was *how* it could be accomplished. This he had never observed. Hence, with his mind set on what he wanted to accomplish, he proceeded to do it in his own rather disorganized way. Although his aim was fairly good, each time he hit the ball it curved to one side and almost invariably ended in the rough. Finally, in desperation the novice inquired of the expert as to the cause of his difficulty. The expert responded by demonstrating and explaining the correct hold on the club which the novice had never before observed. After a number of trials and further tutoring by the expert, the novice was driving his ball successfully. The novice finally discovered that golf is more than dropping a ball into a cup (the end result). He learned that golf is the skilled act of driving a ball, and that the ball can be driven where one wants it to go only by concentrating on the *act of driving* it. He also learned that there is a *best way* to drive a ball and that one is most likely to achieve his end by adopting this "good form" of doing it.

Regardless of the skill you are learning, whether it is ballet dancing, tumbling, archery, typewriting, playing a musical instrument, singing, painting, sculpturing, or horseback riding, remember that in each there is a right way to accomplish what one seeks to accomplish. Discover what this *best way* is. Analyze it carefully. Seek to adapt your responses so that they resemble those of the skilled performer as closely as possible. Concentrate on the skill (the act) and the result that you hope to achieve is sure to follow.

## The Whole-Part Technique

Many of the skills you are now learning are complex and some of them are exceedingly so. Some people insist that the proper way to learn a complex skill is to break it down into its elements, learn each element first as something separate from the others, and then put the parts together as one might assemble the parts of a machine. This may appear to be the logical (engineering) approach to learning but it certainly is not the psychological approach.

One does not learn the swan dive by first running up the diving board 20 or 30 times, then jumping up and down at the end of the board 20 or 30 more times, and so forth until all the parts of the act are practiced. One learns the swan dive by practicing diving—by practicing the *whole act* in its proper sequence.

When learning a complex skill, start by trying to perform the whole, coördinated act first; after a measure of success, then turn to stressing the parts of the total response that require special attention. After you can swim somewhat, then concentrate on the intricacies of the stroke. Remember the principle of "good form" and recognize that good form can be achieved only by diligent attention to details after the general pattern of the response has been set.

Finally, the whole-part approach to learning skills results in stronger motivation which is indispensable to successful learning.

## Set Immediate Goals

In an earlier chapter when we were concerned primarily with ideational learning, we emphasized the importance of setting immediate goals as a technique of learning (see pp. 99–106). The principle of immediate goals is just as important to skilled learning as it is to academic learning. The method of immediate goals also ties in well with the whole-part approach just discussed. After some measure of skill has been established and you have begun to appreciate more fully the nature and importance of some of the details of the total act, single out one or several of these details for special practice. Set for yourself the immediate goal of achieving a measure of perfection in this or that phase of the total response. Each day set new goals as to the details to be practiced or the degree of perfection sought. In this way you will make steady progress toward your ultimate goal in that particular skill.

## Distribute Your Practice

The method of distributed practice was also discussed at some length in an earlier chapter (see pp. 85–89) and therefore it is discussed here only briefly. The reader is urged to refer to the earlier discussion for an account of the nature and advantages of this method.

The practice-rest-practice-rest method of learning poses two questions: How long should the practice periods be? How long should the rest periods between practices be?

*The length of practice periods.* As we noted earlier, specific rules with regard to the length of practice periods cannot be stated. In general, however, the following things appear to be true: When learning skills, shorter rather than longer periods give better results. This is particularly true when the task is a difficult one and when one is in the early stages of learning the skill. The factors that determine the optimum length of the practice period are: the difficulty of the task, the nature of the task, the extent to which learning has progressed, the learner's attitude, and past learning that is related to the present task.

In such a skill as typewriting, a three-minute practice period is considered proper for high school students who are concentrating on securing speed. For college students who are typing continuously at top speed, the practice period should not exceed five minutes. That the length of the practice period does affect speed and accuracy of typing is illustrated by the following results. When the practice period was one minute long, the college students typed perfectly at an average rate of 52 words per minute. When the practice period was lengthened to three minutes, they maintained perfect accuracy but typed only an average of 42 words per minute. When the practice period was extended to five minutes, errorless work was no longer maintained.

Griffith [3] discovered that in the practice of athletic sports a practice period of 20 to 30 minutes was sufficiently long. In fact, he recommends shorter rather than longer periods than these.

[3] C. R. Griffith, *Psychology and Athletics,* New York, Scribner's, 1928, p. 91.

*The length of rest periods.* Laboratory results that could be cited in this connection do not apply directly to everyday life situations. Therefore, we must discover for ourselves what seems to be practical in each case. This we can say, however: short practice periods generally can be followed by short rest pauses and that longer practice periods require longer rest periods. The exigencies of one's daily routine interfere with the setting up of specific principles that can be followed rigidly.

## Put It into Words

Describe the actions involved in a skill if you wish to learn it well. The words used to describe the different phases of the total act serve as cues when you try to reproduce it. Moreover, by putting the action sequence into words you are apt to remember the different phases of the skilled act and their sequence better. Describing the various parts of the skilled response also serves to call one's attention to the number of things that must be done, as well as to their order. Words give acts meaning and meaning always facilitates learning.

The golf "pro" not only demonstrates how to grip a golf club, but he *tells* you that you must hold it so that the "V" formed by the thumb and index finger of your right hand points toward your left shoulder. The driving teacher helps you to learn how to shift gears by *describing* an "H" with each of the three forward gears and the reverse gear located in a certain corner of the letter. The violin teacher *states* how the wrist must be held and what the angle of the arm is when bowing.

Words help us to become aware of *how* the act is performed as well as of *what* is done. Describing what *is done,* especially when what we do is not entirely correct, emphasizes for us our errors and directs our attention to that which is to be avoided in the future. Although this is a negative approach which by itself is of doubtful value, noting errors in one's response often proves to be a valuable supplement to the positive approach of stating that which one must do to achieve proficiency and success.

Therefore, *put into words* what the demonstrator does, or better yet, have him *describe* the various phases of the skill as he demonstrates slowly. *Repeat the description* as you attempt to duplicate the demonstrator's skill. Avoid just looking at what is done. *Talk about it. Describe it.*

### The Use of Rhythm

A skilled response is more than a series of patterned movements—it is also a series of *timed* movements. Timing is very important in such skills as running the hurdles, diving, typewriting, playing a musical instrument, and so on. To facilitate the learning of this timing, rhythm is often introduced by counting, tapping, using a metronome, or some other device that serves as a pacemaker to set the rhythm of the activity. This procedure is used in industry to speed production skills. It is also used by typewriting teachers to aid students to establish a typing rhythm that facilitates speed of typewriting.

*Some observations on the use of rhythm.* Rhythm can be used to good advantage particularly in relatively simple skills in which the cycle of response is repeated over and over again, as in marching in step, skipping rope, rowing a boat, and in calisthenic exercises. To use rhythm effectively, the learner must first achieve a measure of skill especially before an external rhythm is introduced. This is particularly true of the more complex skills such as typewriting. When the typewriting student is still at the stage of hunting for particular keys, rhythm is useless. In the simple skills, such as simple calisthenic exercises, however, rhythm can be introduced early.

When using rhythm with a group of people learning the same skill, all the members of the group must be at about the same stage in their learning, for otherwise the tempo of the rhythm is too slow for some and too fast for others.

*Difficulties with the use of rhythm.* Skills that are single-cycle activities (activities that are not repeated) are seldom facilitated by the use of external rhythms or music. The act of driving a golf ball, for example, is done with a certain complex rhythm, but it is doubtful that one can improve a golfer's skill by having him drive balls to the accompaniment of music. Serving in tennis, pitching and batting in baseball, fly-casting in fishing, and other such skills are illustrations of single-cycle activities in which an external rhythm or music is of doubtful value.

In the case of very complex skills, such as operating a complex bookkeeping machine or check-writing machine, the operator's rhythm is so complex that it would be difficult to impose an externally produced rhythm or music of such tempo that would actually promote skilled performance. This difficulty is also encountered in the case of aesthetic dancing, in which case the music must be composed for the particular dance, and even for the particular dancer, so that the execution of the skilled response is facilitated.

When standard musical compositions are used as an aid in pacing skills, difficulty is encountered in locating music with tempo and rhythm appropriate to the performer's level of skill. This is particularly true when a number of people are engaged in the same activity, as typists in an office or machine operators in a factory. The particular tempo used may increase the typing rate of the slow typists but it may retard the rate of the faster typists. The difficulties of trying to have an appropriate tempo for each typist are insurmountable.

Therefore, we must conclude that in the case of those skills in which an external rhythm or music can be used to good advantage it should be recommended, but we must observe that no such technique is a panacea capable of facilitating all skills.

## Use of Objective Records of Progress

An examination of objective records of one's performance can help greatly in the correction of errors in performance. Some skills, such as tying a necktie or setting a wave in one's hair, are generally learned by observing one's movements in a mirror. This is also common when learning aesthetic dances. Photographs, especially motion pictures (although a bit expensive), can also be used to good advantage in spotting errors in performance, as is often done in football and in basketball.

## The Importance of Practice

All learning comes by doing, and doing means practice. One can never learn a skill and achieve a high level of performance merely by observing another person perform it. One must practice the response himself to get the "feel" of the kinesthetic and other sensory cues that are essential to triggering the response. This can never be gotten by observation alone.

Moreover, since skills involve muscles, some of these muscles need strengthening and this, too, is accomplished only by exercise.

Practice is not to be confused with repetition. Some people think that practice means doing something many times. The mere repetition of an act does not guarantee improvement.

Stop to consider how many thousands of times you have written your name since you started writing it, and then try to imagine how much improvement there has been in the past five years. Has repetition resulted in steady improvement? If you are typical, it is not at all likely. Practice is more than repetition. Practice implies insight into what constitutes ideal performance, a recognition of one's successes and failures, a determination to improve, as well as the repetition of certain acts many times.

How can one facilitate practice? This can be done best by using the skill as often as possible in day-to-day situations. Learn to swim by enjoying a swim often; learn to fly-cast by going fishing often; learn to type by typing all your letters and term papers. Use your skill whenever possible! Use is the chief reason for learning a skill.

## The T-S-D-P Method

The *tell-show-do-praise* method of learning embraces a number of the things that have been discussed in various parts of this chapter.

Apply this method by having the demonstrator of the skill first *describe* it very carefully for you—*tell* you step by step what must be done. If his description is a good one, you can learn much as to the sequence of the activities, the external cues to be noted, the names that are generally applied to different phases of the skill (if names are used), and the goal which one is striving to achieve. Do not stop with this verbal description of the skill no matter how excellent it may be. Take the next step and insist on a careful *demonstration,* preferably accompanied by a repetition of the description.

The third step in this method of learning a skill is to try to *do* what has just been described and demonstrated. Do it yourself! Remember to *describe the steps* as you attempt to duplicate each, for this is an essential part of the method. Ask the demonstrator to correct your errors in description as well as performance. In this way, your attention will be called specifically to the parts of the skill that are incorrectly performed.

If your instructor is a competent teacher of skills, he will follow each performance with some word of praise or commendation that will strengthen your drive to try again.

Repeat this whole performance a number of times, each time laying stress on improving your *verbal description* as well as your performance. Learn to use the *tell-show-do-praise* method each time you learn a new skill.

## SPEED AND ACCURACY

A common question raised when learning certain skills is: is it best to emphasize *speed* or *accuracy* first? In the case of some skills, this is not a problem because emphasis is entirely on accuracy and not at all on speed. This is true of painting, sketching, engineering drawing, fly-casting, sculpturing, making stained glass windows, cabinet-making, and other such skills. In such skills as these the level of excellence and the quality of that which is produced are important. In other skills, however, such as typewriting, operating business machines, hurdling in track, and similar skills, both speed and accuracy are important.

The one skill in which the speed-versus-accuracy problem has been studied intensively is typewriting. The Gilbreths, Dvorak, and other researchers in this problem agree that in learning typing one must emphasize *technique,* not good copy, in the beginning. Therefore, one starts to learn the skill by learning the correct motions with emphasis on the speed with which they are made, for accuracy is secondary at this time.

The old notion of first learning to make accurate responses and then gradually speeding up the activity is no longer held. The reason for discarding this view is that a fast response differs from a slow one in other ways than speed. When walking at a fast pace, one does not walk the same (except more quickly) as one does when walking at a slow pace. Throwing a "fast" ball is not the same as throwing a "slow" ball. Likewise, when making fast strokes in typing, one does not hit the keys as hard nor curl the fingers in the same way as when typing slowly. Because of these differences between fast and slow responses, it is best, when learning a skill in which speed is important, to execute each response as *quickly as possible right from the beginning,* and thus avoid the necessity of changing the form of the response later in order to achieve greater speed. In fact, it is desirable to respond at one's *maximum speed* as early as possible with little fear that this will have an adverse effect on accuracy. After the speed aspect of the skill has been established, attention should be given to the improvement of accuracy.

# 7.

# Getting the Most Out of Class Work

## ATTITUDES ARE PRIMARY

### The Nature of Attitudes

Attitudes are an intimate part of us and of our daily experience, and we are well acquainted with them. Although we feel rather certain that we know what attitudes are, a brief examination of the concept will serve to define our thinking.

Attitudes are ways of behaving toward some object, person, social group or institution, in such ways as to indicate our approval or disapproval of them. Sometimes this behavior is verbal, as when we say that we like the British people or hate the Communists; at other times, it is a gesture, as when we wrinkle our nose at the mention of garlic or shake our head on hearing an ancient joke badly told.

Attitudes have an object; they represent a relationship between yourself and something that is not yourself. Perhaps you say that you "like" your roommate but "detest" mathematics; that you "simply adore" (if you are a girl) your English teacher, or are "just crazy" about high-fidelity recordings. These attitudes are not just responses to things or to people; they are positive or negative responses—approach or withdrawal—and they indicate approval or disapproval. In other words, the relationship between you and the object of your attitude is a value relationship.

Finally, attitudes represent a rather fixed or habitual way of responding toward things and, hence, they make for consistency in our behavior. Some attitudes, however, are undesirable and they too are consistent, well-learned, and difficult to change. Yet to get the most out of our classwork they may need to be changed. Let us examine the kinds of attitudes that do make for academic success.

## Attitude and Academic Success

Life is full of beginnings. You as a freshman are on one of those thresholds of beginning. Entering a new course marks a beginning; enrolling as a "prep" student for a given occupation or profession is also a beginning. Will you succeed in that which you are now beginning?

Several factors combine to answer this question. There is, for example, your past training and preparation for the course or program you are about to enter. The degree of your mastery of those essential prerequisites for the present course is of obvious importance to present success. Entering a course in college mathematics with an inadequate grasp of the fundamentals of elementary algebra is almost certain to spell failure. Then, too, there is the matter of native ability and intelligence. Some people just lack what it takes to understand and master certain courses. As for doing something about inadequate preparation, the possibility is there but the likelihood may be doubtful; as for natural endowment, there is no substitute for lack of aptitude—not even determination.

Having the prerequisites and the necessary abilities is still no sure guarantee of academic success. Another ingredient is essential, namely, *attitude*. I have seen not a few intellectually able and academically well-qualified students fail courses they did not need to fail due to poor attitudes toward themselves, their work, and their professors. On the other hand, not infrequently, one sees much less well-qualified students with average endowments who do succeed moderately well because of wholesome attitudes toward themselves and their own capabilities, toward that which they are learning, and toward their professors. It is this latter matter, the matter of attitude, that you certainly can do somehing about —that you can do something about now! What are these attitudes that make for academic success?

### Adopt a Mature Attitude

Maturity cannot be put on voluntarily like a coat. Maturity is a way of acting and thinking that comes as a result of learning, and for some students this learning is especially difficult. The process of maturing, from the standpoint of personality, is not one of merely metamorphosing from the stature of an infant to that of an adult; rather it is a matter of making one's world *group-centered* rather than *self-centered*. A mature attitude is evident when a person recognizes that there are certain standards of behavior that are for the common good, and when he demonstrates his willingness to conform to these standards even though he must sacrifice some of his own individuality to do so. All else stems from these two things.

Therefore, the person with a mature attitude is *willing to conform* to the rules and regulations of the social group of which he is a part, even though he may chafe a bit now and then when doing so. In the classroom the mature student accepts assignments, even though they do not always suit his convenience, completes them by the due date, and presents them in the form requested. In other words, he sacrifices some of his own individuality so that the other members of the group and the instructor may also enjoy some of their individuality.

The mature person *accepts responsibility*. He accepts membership in a class as a contract to do what the instructor asks him to do, not because he is doing it for the instructor, but because he is accepting the instructor's leadership in the course, and because he wants to learn as much as he can from the course.

The mature person is a *self-reliant person*. He does not expect someone else to do all his thinking and deciding for him. He stands on his own two feet. Moreover, he accepts the consequences that follow an occasional bad judgment and refuses to shift the responsibility by placing the blame on someone else. When a student with a mature attitude gets a low grade or fails a course, he accepts it as due to his failure rather than due to the professor's bias, his inadequate tests, or dull lectures.

The mature person *puts first things first*. His values are determined by group standards rather than by his own whims. He has perspective. He appreciates the long-time value of preparing an assignment, participating in a debate, or doing a necessary job well as more important than seeing the latest movie or participating in a midnight poker game just to be "one of the boys."

## Some Indicators of Immaturity

College teachers observe a variety of behavior and attitudes that indicate the presence of immaturity in their students. A common one is the request for private concessions—postponing a test, allowing more time to prepare a report or write a term paper, and so forth. And what justifications are given for requesting these concessions? They are such as these: A fellow is required to help with the decorations for a fraternity party, or he must prepare for a test in another course. A girl just must go to a neighboring city to shop, or extend the length of her week-end visit to her boy friend's home.

It is true that there are times when it is perfectly proper for a student to ask a professor to make a concession because circumstances are such that any fair-minded person would recognize the merits of one's case; but to request concessions to satisfy whims, or to gain trivial and selfish pleasures shows a lack of realism. After all, practically every time a professor is asked to make a concession, he is inconvenienced; and you may be sure that every time you ask for a concession, several other students have asked for one also. The next time you want to make such a request, just stop to think what the situation would be if everyone in the class insisted that his private request be granted.

Another indicator of immaturity is the failure to meet appointments. Every professor is glad to help students and to discuss with them their problems. This he regards as part of his task as a teacher. However, when a student fails to meet one or several appointments just because he "forgot" or "overslept," you may rest assured that that professor's attitude toward that student has been definitely affected. Even though he is willing to give generously of his time, he does have things to do other than to wait for an undependable and irresponsible student.

A third indicator is present-mindedness and lack of planning. The student who is so absorbed in himself and his present gratification that he cannot anticipate his need for the future shows immaturity. This is his usual excuse: "I just didn't have time."

A final indicator of immaturity is irresponsibility in carrying a job through to completion. I have observed students who agreed to administer objective tests or demonstrate an experiment at certain specified times, who reported for one or two of the periods and neglected to do so for the remaining ones without notifying anyone of their intention to quit, and without making an explanation or offering an apology later. Such behavior is immature behavior.

### Class Behavior as an Indicator of Attitude

One's classroom behavior indicates one's attitude toward the course and the instructor. Here are several such indicators and their psychological implications. The very *place you choose to sit* on the first and succeeding days that you enter the course indicates something about your attitude. Students who choose to sit in the last row of chairs or seats indicate that they are trying to get as far away from the professor and the course as possible and still be a part of the course. Somehow they think that they are more secure when there is much that separates them from the instructor. The person who chooses to sit at the end of the row or near the door shows that he is timid and uncertain of himself. He wants to be a part of the class, but is afraid. The student who elects to sit toward the front or near the center of the classroom indicates that he has come to participate in the activities of the course and that he expects to remain a member of the class.

Sleeping in a class is a very obvious way of telling the instructor that his course is very dull and uninteresting. Generally, the students who are convinced that this is true of a course head for the last row of seats where they think they can relax and sleep without disturbing anyone and in com-

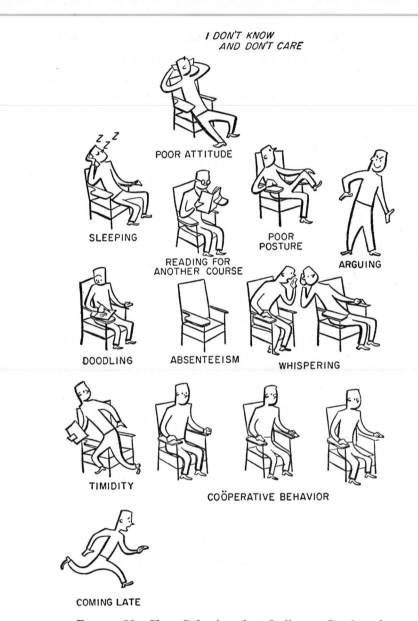

FIGURE 33. Class Behavior that Indicates Good and Poor Attitudes.

plete security. It is true that they hurt no one—no one, that is, but themselves.

Reading a text used in another course, while attending a class, tells the instructor that the student regards the material presented in his course as so unimportant and trivial that he knows he is making much better use of his time by preparing for another course than by participating in this one. This student indicates bluntly that his only reason for attending this class is to avoid an absence.

Bad body posture, as when a student sits on the small of his back, and unfocused eyes indicate a lack of attention and of interest in the course. Usually this student is daydreaming about something far removed from the content of the course, and his attention is at very low ebb or completely nonexistent.

Looking continually at the arm of one's chair, being pre-occupied with an object of some sort, or doodling in one's notebook indicates either a lack of preparation and a fear of being asked to respond in class, or a marked lack of interest in the subject. It is not uncommon to find that this type of behavior indicates both of these things.

Sometimes a bolder student with poor class attitudes argues with the instructor, oftentimes facetiously, with the sole purpose of confusing the issues, annoying the instructor, and inflating his own ego because he dares to challenge the instructor. This student is more interested in "putting the instructor in his place" than he is in learning more about the subject by honest debate. Also, telling the professor that the course is "uninteresting" or "impractical," or that the textbook is "poorly written" indicates more often than not that the student is rationalizing, especially when the quality of his own work is not good.

Finally, irregular attendance and frequent lateness when there is no legitimate reason for either, indicate attitude.

When there is a valid reason for either, the student, for his own welfare, should discuss the matter with the instructor lest the instructor react to the lateness and frequent absence as indicating indifference.

### Reasons for Poor Attitudes

First we must recognize (and some students will gladly) that not all teaching is high quality teaching. Teachers, like other specialists, differ in the quality of their performance. Furthermore, the good teacher, like the good athlete and the good musician, is not at his best each day. No one who performs daily and for nine or more months a year will give a top-notch performance *every time*. Nevertheless, most professors strive continually to improve the quality of their teaching. Although a poor lecture does generate poor attitudes, students are too often prone to rationalize their own shortcomings as due to the professor's real or imagined inadequacies. Hence, they feel justified in exhibiting a poor attitude. "After all," they reason, "our poor attitude is not due to anything we have done; it is the professor's fault that we do so poorly."

What can one do about this? How can you improve student-professor relationships? For one thing, you can avoid doing some or all of the things discussed in the preceding section, and concentrate on doing as many of the things discussed in the remaining sections of this chapter as possible. Help yourself to learn more by helping your professor to be a more successful teacher. To make a class discussion successful and rewarding, he needs your help as well as you need his guidance. Teaching is a coöperative venture which is seldom if ever successful when one member of the team is reactionary, or indifferent and passive.

A second factor that hinders academic success is the conviction, held by not a few students, that the instructor is an adversary rather than a friend. This view, developed largely during high-school days, stems from the fact that assignments then become longer and more difficult, and that teachers insist on higher standards of performance, thus making life somewhat unpleasant for the student. Consequently, the student is prone to fix his resentment on the teacher "who is the cause of all the trouble." It is the teacher who is thought to be at fault rather than one's own lack of legitimately required achievement. This hostility toward the teacher easily becomes a firmly established attitude that transfers readily when one enters college where the demands on one are even higher than they were in high school. Hence, the old animus comes quickly to the fore and the student falls back into his old pattern of resistance.

Analyze your actions and your attitudes objectively. If you have a hostile attitude toward a particular course, try to determine the cause of your attitude. Concentrate on correcting your own poor attitudes; stop resisting the instructor. Adopt deliberately and with intention a much more favorable attitude than you have at present and discover for yourself that it does pay dividends in greater learning and much more enjoyment.

Another factor that hinders good attitude is emphasis on grades rather than on learning and accomplishment. The current emphasis on grades is not entirely a student fault; our educational system is built around this type of evaluation. Because of this emphasis, grades do become goals, and failure to earn high grades results in pain—pain that stems from the displeasure of parents and the lack of recognition or the outright ridicule of one's peer group. Soon this pain comes to be anticipated and feared, which means that anxiety develops— anxiety lest one do less well than he desires or should do. As anxiety mounts, the drive to achieve tends to be lessened, and as the drive to achieve decreases the quality of one's performance declines. This, then, generates even more anxiety, and so the cycle continues. This psychology of frustration and anxiety accounts for the "petrified feeling" that some students have when they are required to take mathematics, or a foreign language, or some other required subject.

Become acquainted with the psychology of anxiety and the way it operates. Concentrate on learning and achievement rather than on grades. Recognize that as a college student you must make the mastery of knowledge and techniques your goal, and that only as you do this are your attitudes likely to improve.

## BE A PARTICIPANT

A good attitude is essential for wholesome participation in classroom work but it is no sure guarantee that one will participate. When one becomes a participant in a course, he takes a second step (good attitude is the first) in the direction of achievement. Take this second step; increase your chances of learning more with less effort. How can one become a participant? Here are several specific ways.

### Choose a Favorable Location

Where one sits in a classroom determines in part the likelihood with which he will participate. The last row in any classroom generally seems to be so far away from the instructor that participation in class activity is difficult. Therefore, students who occupy the last row, because of their detached feeling, are more apt to participate in nonclass activities, to make whispered comments, and to do other things that are distracting, and thus make it difficult for the interested student who sits there to participate. Moreover, the person who sits in the back of the classroom often feels that there are so many people in front of him, and that he therefore will have to talk so loudly to be heard, that due to his embarrassment he is reluctant to respond at all. Avoid sitting in the last row of chairs if you wish to participate in the activities of the class.

Sitting in the fringes of a group also makes for less group feeling or a feeling of belonging, and, hence, the student who sits in the fringe of the class often finds it more difficult to participate.

The best position in the classroom is near the center of the row of chairs and in one of the forward rows. In this position one has more in-group feeling with the other members of the class and a closer rapport with the teacher. The timid student does not need to speak as loudly to be heard, and the self-conscious student is less aware of the number of students who are sitting behind him. Therefore, if possible, choose this favorable position in the classroom that will make it easier for you to participate in class activities and discussions.

## Start Participating Early

Enter into the class discussion on the first day or certainly during the first week. Beware of postponing participation until a later date, or after you are acquainted with your fellow students, the instructor, and the content of the course. To do this means that the chances that you will ever participate are small.

Supposing you say nothing during the first six weeks of the course and then finally you get up sufficient courage to make a comment. How are your classmates apt to react to you? Are they going to be overjoyed that finally you have spoken, or are they going to look at you with wonder and amazement that even you have an idea on the subject! You may even hear someone whisper, "Who is he? We have never heard from him before!" As a result of this first, delayed venture in participation, you are quite likely to experience self-consciousness and embarrassment. If your emotional experience is intense enough, you may never participate again. Remember it is much harder to "break the ice" after six weeks of nonparticipation than it is on the first day or during the first week. Establish the reputation of being an early participant and you will find it easier to participate with each group experience.

## Ways One May Participate

*Recite material you have learned.* This is perhaps the easiest type of participation since it is merely a matter of recalling what has been learned while preparing the day's assignment. Therefore, the timid student who finds participation difficult and embarrassing can use this method of participation to good advantage.

*Report relevant experiences.* This method of participation is somewhat more difficult than the above method because one must have insight into the relevance of his experiences as well as the ability to recall and present them. Caution must be used when relating personal experiences lest one fall into the error of just reporting interesting experiences that have little or no bearing on the topic under discussion. Each experience should illustrate a point, point up an issue, or raise a question.

*Ask questions.* This method is also often difficult to use, for pertinent questions grow only out of the knowledge one has of the subject. Ask questions that reveal your insight into the problem under consideration and your knowledge of that which you have studied. Avoid using questions as a short cut to answers you should have discovered during your prepara-

FIGURE 34. Ways in Which One Can Participate in
Classroom Activities.

tion for the class period. Remember that the nature and quality of your questions indicate the quality of your thinking. For this reason, even asking an unanswerable question shows your grasp of the implications in the problem under consideration. A final value of asking questions is that it stimulates your own thinking and thereby enhances your interest in the course.

*Make an agreement with the professor.* Some students want to participate in class discussions but are so hesitant and self-conscious that they cannot bring themselves to the point of actual participation. Each time such a person has an idea to express, he delays so long that someone else makes his point before he musters the courage to speak. And if he is called on unexpectedly, he is generally so frightened that he can think of nothing to say.

There is a solution for this problem. The student must discuss his difficulty with his professor and indicate that he is willing and anxious to participate but unable to overcome his fear of reciting. Having indicated his problem and admitted his weakness, he must then ask the professor to give him an opportunity to recite and to help him overcome his difficulty.

As a college professor with more than 30 years of experience, I have made the following agreement with many timid students as a means of helping them to overcome their timidity. I first agree to call on the student at least once during each discussion period, but I at the same time assure him that there are certain other things that I shall do to protect and help him. I promise to give him some warning (usually by looking at him) that I am about to call on him. I further assure him that I shall so phrase my question that a brief answer ("yes" or "no" in the beginning) will be adequate, and finally I agree that if he shows hesitation or inability to answer the question, I shall supply the answer for him. In any case, I agree never to embarrass the student, and in effect guarantee success. After a few such experiences, and as the student gains self-confidence, I ask him more difficult questions and delay my rescue. The genuinely sincere student generally gains confidence rapidly with this treatment, and in a short time is volunteering information and asking questions on his own initiative.

If you are afraid to participate in a class discussion, ask your professor to do this for you, and thus bolster your self-confidence, increase your participation, and enhance your success in the course.

## BE A COÖPERATOR

Be a coöperator and increase your academic success. There are a number of ways in which a student can coöperate with an instructor for the mutual benefit of both. Some of these we have already discussed, such as wholesome attitude and active participation. Full coöperation, however, means still other things.

### Exceed Minimum Requirements

Minimum achievement is mediocrity. To succeed commendably in anything, one must go well beyond the stated minimum. If a professor asks you to write a term paper of at least 2,000 words, or to read a minimum of 5 references out of a list of 15, or to solve 3 or more problems out of a dozen, do more than the minimum number specified.

I have many students who, having difficulty with a course, state very honestly (sometimes naïvely) and with the light of triumph in their eye, that they have read the *entire chapter* assigned, as though this were a very worthy achievement. Without a doubt, they have *read* the chapter (once); but have they recited its contents, overlearned its chief points, put the material into their own words, and reread sections several times with a different purpose each time? Merely reading the chapter is the least one can do, and one's least effort never results in genuine accomplishment.

Remember that minimal compliance with an assignment indicates that you are on the verge of failure, not at the acme of success.

### Volunteer Something Extra

One way to get the most out of a course, and incidentally to develop a favorable relationship with the instructor, is to go well beyond the assignment given you and do something extra. Set for yourself and carry to completion self-initiated projects that stimulate your interest, enrich your experience, and extend your knowledge. Refrain from just doing a larger quantity of something (five extra problems in mathematics), even though this has some merit; do something that requires initiative and planning. Illustrate various reactions to frustration by drawing a series of cartoons (for psychology); make a relief map of a battleground (for history); construct a model showing a cross section of various strata of rock (for geology); interview a group of consumers (for economics); or make a public opinion poll (for political science). Do something extra that will be a challenge and a joy. Such extra effort always pays off in faculty good-will as well as in knowledge.

### Comply with Routine Requirements

Small things often make a great difference. Coöperate in the small things as well as the large, for small things sometimes prove to be much more important than they seem. Be on time to class each day and be present at each meeting of the class. Do not take the "cuts" you think you are entitled to in a course. Present term papers, experimental reports, projects, and other assigned things to the instructor on or before the due date. Do not request extensions of time and other personal favors just because you have failed to plan well. Note this well: coöperation is always measured in terms of compliance.

### Look and Act Interested

No argument is necessary to convince you that you cannot be angry or depressed when you are laughing heartily. Behaving in a given way not only precludes the possibility of certain experiences, but it also makes certain other experiences possible. That is why looking and acting interested when you are a member of a class does generate interest.

According to our definition of interest presented earlier (see pp. 37–39), any student who *responds positively* to the work done in a course, who seeks to *derive pleasure* from it, who is willing to *spend time thinking* about it, and who *works diligently* is certain to be interested in it. Be not deceived; interest is not effortless! One must work at something to be interested in it. Give this view of interest a fair trial. Prove to yourself that it does work.

## TAKE USEFUL NOTES

### The Purposes of Note-Taking

Why should one take notes on an instructor's lecture or on a class discussion? In general, there are two chief reasons: (1) the taking of notes facilitates learning; and (2) the notes taken are the tools used in the fixation of learning. Let us consider each of these points further.

*The taking of notes facilitates learning.* When one takes notes he *attends* to what is said and done; he also *analyzes* and *thinks* rapidly about what he sees and hears; and finally, he *records* his observations. Attending to, analyzing, and doing something about a class lecture or discussion means that the student is actively engaged in those activities that are essential to effective learning. Since note-taking forces the student to do these things, notetaking facilitates learning.

*Notes taken are tools in the fixation of learning.* Notes are the cues that *stimulate recall.* A word or a brief statement in one's notes stimulates the recall of a line of reasoning, the background for an event, the cause of a situation or condition, or the approach to a problem. Hence, notes are valuable symbols that aid recall.

Furthermore, notes are a valuable *check on the accuracy of one's recall.* Did the professor present a certain point as of *major* or *minor* importance? What was the sequence of events that precipitated the strike? Your notes should answer these questions and set you straight on the matters of which you are not certain.

Notes are also valuable guides when using self-recitation, which is essential for effective learning as we have pointed out before. They also serve as a prompter when one has a tendency to short-circuit a line of thought or the solution to a problem.

Finally, notes, being an epitome and a résumé, make certain points stand out in bold relief in comparison to others and thus help one grasp the significance and value of some points in comparison to others. This latter point is often especially important when preparing for a test or an examination.

## How to Take Notes

Taking notes is not a leisurely matter; one must keep going to keep pace with the lecturer or the class discussion. One must learn to *listen attentively* (since a repetition is unlikely), to *judge and decide quickly* as to the nature of the point made, and to *record briefly* the pith of what is said. To do this well and to continue doing this for an hour or more, means that one must *learn the skill* of note-taking. This ability to take notes well comes only as the result of learning. Therefore, learn the technique early in your college career.

*Learn to listen.* Spend more time listening than writing, for when you are attending to writing you are not attending to listening, and, hence, while you are writing one thing you may miss one or several others that are also important.

*Put the thought into your own words.* Notes are not supposed to be a stenographic copy; they are cues to ideas. As cues they will serve you best if they are your own rather than someone else's. Putting an idea into your own words means that you are doing more than transcribing it; you are making it your own—you are learning it.

*Epitomize.* Reduce every complex idea to as few words as possible; sometimes, even a single word that has a great deal of meaning for you is sufficient. Cut through the maze of details and discover the heart of the idea and record it. After you discover the central theme of the thought or line of reasoning, many of the details will be remembered without effort.

### Kinds of Notes

One cannot always take notes in exactly the same way. The content of the course, the procedures used, and the habits and preferences of the instructor are factors that determine whether your notes are of the *outline type* or the *sentence summary* type. Sometimes, this will differ even from day to day in the same course because of variations in the professor's procedures.

If the instructor follows closely a prepared outline when

lecturing, and if he indicates major divisions and subpoints, as some do, then your notes should resemble rather closely

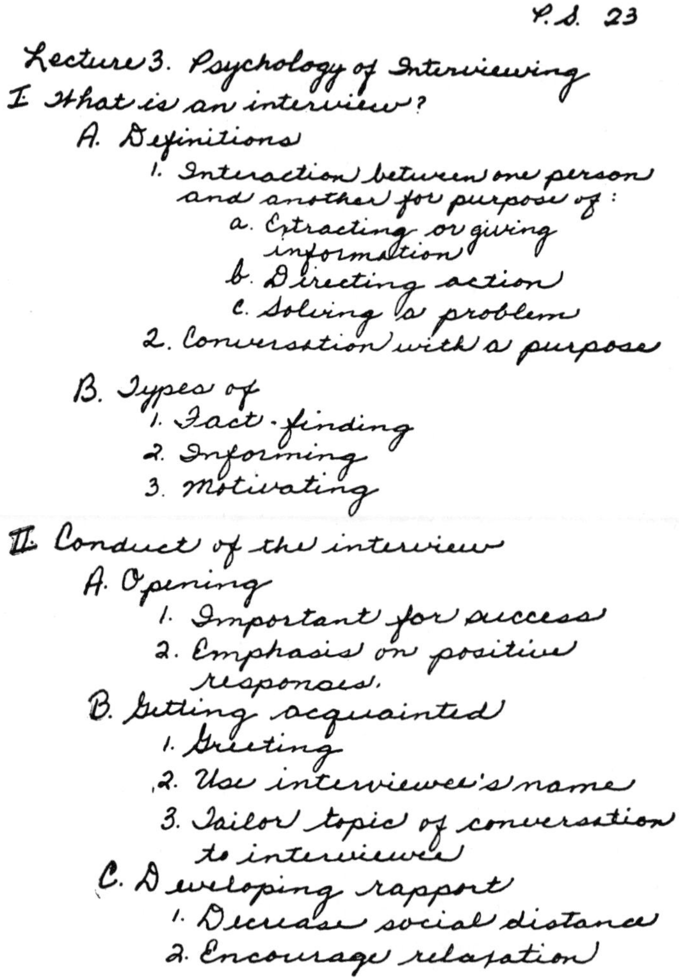

*P. S. 23*

Lecture 3. Psychology of Interviewing
I  What is an interview?
  A. Definitions
    1. Interaction between one person
       and another for purpose of:
       a. Extracting or giving
          information
       b. Directing action
       c. Solving a problem
    2. Conversation with a purpose

  B. Types of
    1. Fact-finding
    2. Informing
    3. Motivating

II  Conduct of the interview
  A. Opening
    1. Important for success
    2. Emphasis on positive
       responses.
  B. Getting acquainted
    1. Greeting
    2. Use interviewee's name
    3. Tailor topic of conversation
       to interviewee
  C. Developing rapport
    1. Decrease social distance
    2. Encourage relaxation

FIGURE 35. A Specimen of Notes Taken in Outline Form.

his outline. Some instructors even put such an outline on the board, an outline which the student can follow and fill in details to whatever extent he sees fit. Other instructors be-

Juvenile Delinquency (Cont.) Soc. 19

Social factors:

 The study of delinquency areas indicates delinquency is very frequent in areas in transition.

 See; C. R. Shaw: Delinquency Areas.

Areas in transition are of two types:

 Displacement of residential areas by commerce which increases day-time population, contact with strangers, uncertainty, etc.

 Population changes: influx into neighborhood of people with different cultural, racial and national backgrounds.

Culture conflicts between generations as a social factor.

 Some conflict is natural.

 Children of immigrants have more conflicts.

FIGURE 36. A Specimen of Sentence-Summary Notes.

lieve that this is providing too much of a crutch for the student and that he is doing work which the student should learn to do for himself.

Some instructors present their material by use of a discussion procedure rather than a formal lecture. In this case, the student finds it much more difficult to discover an outline in the material discussed, even though one is used, and he must resort to the sentence summary method of taking notes. The danger in the sentence summary method is that too often the student does little more than record isolated statements. When using this method, one must try to relate the various statements recorded so that the development of the idea is obvious, and so that the value and importance of the various statements are in some way indicated. Some combination of the two methods (outline and sentence summary) often proves practical. When one is not certain of the outline followed by the lecturer, one should indicate the relative importance of items by using the usual numbers, letters, and indentations as much as possible, and then use the sentence summary method where the relative importance of points is less clear.

### Edit Your Notes

The time taken to edit one's notes is time well spent providing it is done with the following objectives.

The best way to edit one's notes is to rewrite them *as soon after taking them as possible,* and certainly no later than *the same day they were taken.* Early editing is important because the longer the delay the more is forgotten and the stronger is the tendency to abbreviate and short-circuit. The purpose of editing notes is to *enrich them with details* that are still remembered at the time of editing and which could not be recorded at the time the original notes were taken. Editing gives one an opportunity to complete one's notes with items still remembered on the first day but soon forgotten if they are not recorded soon.

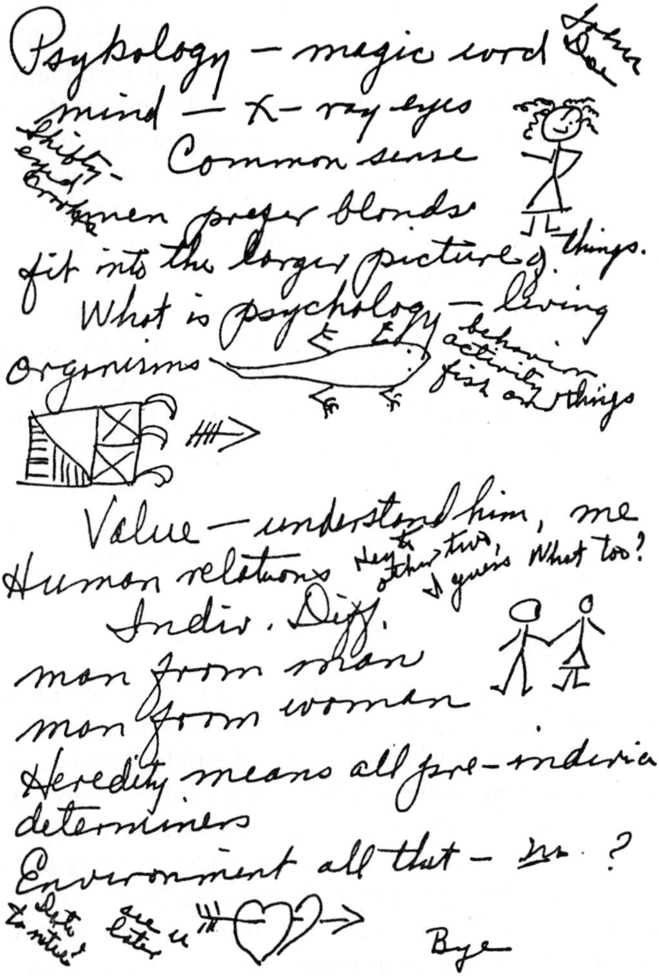

FIGURE 37. A Specimen of What Notes Should Not Look Like.

Editing also gives one the opportunity to *improve the organization* of the notes, especially when the sentence summary method is used, and to *indicate* more accurately the *importance* of various items. Diagrams of apparatus used and of schematic representations of ideas can be labeled more adequately at one's leisure so that their meanings are not lost. All this does much to improve the quality of one's notes so that they are much more meaningful when used for review purposes. Rewriting not only improves the quality of the content but also the legibility of the notes. This too is important, for notes are of little value if they cannot be read several weeks after they are taken.

A final, and I think most important, value that comes from editing and rewriting notes is that in doing so one *relates and recites* the material at a most advantageous time —a time when much of the material is still rather clearly remembered. This is the reason for my insistence that the editing be done the same day the notes are taken. This advantage will never be yours if you postpone editing notes for several days or weeks. *Editing* results in *better notes* and in *more effective learning*.

## Sundry Suggestions

Type your notes or use ink when you rewrite them. Keep your notes for all courses in one notebook (separated by dividers) so that you will always have the right notebook and know where your notes are. Number the pages of notes for each course consecutively and identify each with a symbol (*Sp* for speech, *Ps* for psychology) so that they can be sorted easily should they ever become disarranged. Never mix doodles and notes. Do not rely on copying another student's notes, for they are never as meaningful to you as they are to someone else, and as your own notes are to you.

# 8.

# *The Importance of Favorable Surroundings*

THE three chief essentials that determine whether we learn more with less effort are: (1) the attitudes we hold and the strength of our drive or intention to learn; (2) the techniques of learning that we employ; (3) the physical conditions that surround us while we are learning. Each of these factors is important. In this chapter, we shall consider the third factor, namely, the ways in which our immediate environment contributes to or hinders our learning.

## A TIME AND A PLACE FOR STUDY

### The Time Schedule

To accomplish the most, regardless of the job, one must be orderly in his attack on the task. This means, among other things, that one must time his activities. For some people, this is very difficult because they have not disciplined themselves to meet deadlines—they are not *time-conscious.* Yet, our society constantly demands that we time our activities, whether it is catching a bus, meeting a class, or presenting a term report.

*Timing takes planning.* If one is to plan wisely, it means that one must know what is required of him. He must recognize his own assets and limitations from the standpoint of accomplishment, gauge future accomplishment in terms of past achievement, and anticipate the exigencies that may arise to hinder progress. Having noted and evaluated each of these factors, he is ready to plan a time schedule.

*A time schedule is a guide.* A time schedule is an aid and not a taskmaster that you must serve as a slave. It should always be something of which you are the master, and which you use voluntarily as an aid to self-discipline. A time schedule is merely an intelligent guess that you make as to what you can accomplish so that you can get the most done and still have a maximum amount of freedom and leisure. Therefore, approach the task of making a time schedule as though it were something to facilitate your work and increase your freedom.

*A time schedule must be flexible.* Since a time schedule is a self-imposed plan of action, it can be changed from time to time to meet present needs and exigencies. One can never anticipate his future so accurately that he can determine exactly how and when every detail can and must be done. Unexpected things do arise; demands on one sometimes are heavier than anticipated. Moreover, we ourselves are not always up to par and hence cannot always carry out a predetermined plan. These and other things, therefore, require us to change our time schedules from time to time. Beware of making too many changes, however. Consider carefully the results of each change. Be aware of making changes that just provide more release from work and that hinder or make it impossible for you to get essential work done. To do this means that the whole value of the time schedule is lost.

When conditions require a change in your time schedule,

trade time rather than just steal it. If on a particular day your English or German assignments are exceptionally heavy, borrow time from the period assigned to science in which you have an assignment lighter than usual. In any case, show discretion; accept your obligations; reach your goals.

*How to construct a time schedule.* Make a calendar on a large sheet of paper with the days of the week across the top and the hours of the day indicated along the left-hand margin starting with the hour when you arise in the morning. Make a cross-hatch by drawing lines so that each period of each day is represented by an oblong box. Write into these boxes your *schedule of courses first,* because your life should revolve around your school work. Abbreviate your course designations (Eng. 101, Hist. 110) and write them in with red pencil, for they are red-letter periods in your schedule. Next list *periods of fixed employment* that you have, for they will take time out from studying. Other fixed times that are a part of your schedule, such as meals, choir or band rehearsals, club meetings, church, and so forth, must also be indicated, even though some of these are less demanding on your time than some other things are. They all are a part of a well-rounded life and therefore must be listed.

The remaining spaces in the time schedule, and they must not be too few in number, must be allotted to study, recreation and social activities, and to meeting personal needs such as rest. Each of these things is important; none can be slighted.

Here are several guiding principles; use them when planning study time:

*Use daytime hours.* As much as possible, use your daytime hours for studying. Daytime is always a preferred time for working in our society; hence, most people are employed during the day. Work when others work. During the day our attitude toward work is more positive; generally, we have more energy and are less fatigued. Take advantage of this by studying during the day.

We usually start our day in the morning. Start your day right by putting first things first, and get your studying done as early as possible. Some students believe, although quite incorrectly, that there is virtue in studying late at night and in burning the "midnight fluorescent." The time of day or night one studies is not what makes one a scholar; it is *how one works* that makes the difference.

It is customary to seek recreation in the evening. Therefore, get as much of your work done during the day as possible and you will enjoy your evening leisure more. Avoid being a martyr to the books because you have frittered away your daylight hours doing things that are neither rewarding nor enjoyable.

*Study after a class.*   This may sound unreasonable to you. Why study, you may ask, after a class? Shouldn't one rather study just before going to a class? Generally, students believe that it is better to study just before going to a class. This is because they often do not learn what is assigned well enough to remember it long. There is also the danger when studying shortly beforehand that one will allow an insufficient amount of time to prepare adequately. It is true that one should *review* just before going to class, but he *should not do the bulk of his studying then.*

Studying after class has these advantages. Many of the ideas and explanations given during the class period are still fresh in one's memory and, hence, they stimulate further thinking when reviewed. It is also an ideal time to rewrite or edit one's class notes, as we pointed out in the last chapter. Perseveration, the tendency to continue what we are doing, also is given an opportunity to operate and to fixate what has just been learned. Furthermore, we are generally less crowded for time just after a class, and we develop less emotion and anxiety with reference to the course and our success in it. Finally, because we are studying with less pressure, we enjoy our work more and learn more with less effort.

*Use the bits of time.* A period of time, no matter how short, can be used to advantage. Use short-time periods for doing the bit things, such as typing another page of a manuscript, looking up several new words in a dictionary, translating another paragraph of French, or reciting a conjugation. One does not have to have a large block of time to get something done. Not all of one's work can be done bit by bit, it is true, but the utilization of short-time periods can add up to a sizeable accomplishment, and generally with little apparent effort. Use the minutes and they will give you hours, some of which you can use for recreation and personal enjoyment.

## The Place Makes a Difference

We learn to associate certain acts and certain experiences with certain places. To meditate or pray, we go to a church or retire to the privacy of our room; to be entertained, we go to a theater or to a fair. The place puts us into the mood for doing or experiencing certain things. So also, the place in which we study should put us into the mood for doing one thing—studying.

Some businessmen recognize the importance of this principle of the attitude-provoking nature of the work place to such an extent that when at their desks they refuse to do anything but that which pertains to their business. The desk, for them, comes to be the cue for one thing only—business. You will be wise if you too will adopt this attitude so that each time you sit down to your study table it will release in you studying activities and nothing else.

Generally, all of one's study cannot be done in just one place. Some work must be done in the library, and other work must be done in a laboratory. Sometimes there is insufficient time to return to one's room or home, where one generally studies, each time one has some free time. Therefore, one must learn to study in various places. It may be a favorite table or corner in a library; or it may be an unused classroom where one has privacy and quiet. Finding such a place that can be used again and again is desirable, for after a time one comes to have an "at home" feeling in that place, and if one has a definite set to study when there, much can be accomplished.

## THE STUDY DESK

### Placement of the Desk

In the preceding section, we stressed the importance of having a definite place to study. In this section, we shall consider the placement of the study desk.

It is possible that you have little choice in this matter, for the floor plan of your room may be such that there is only one spot available for a study desk, and this spot may be good or bad from the standpoint of psychological principles. It is also possible that your room is equipped with a dual study desk which is so constructed that you must face your roommate each time you study, whether you want to or not. Some modern dormitories have built-in study desks that may or may not be properly placed. If you have such a study desk and it is not well placed, you have no choice but to accept it.

*Desirable placement.* The most desirable placement of a study desk is against a wall so that the student faces the wall, yet close enough to a window so that one can take advantage of the daylight without being distracted by that which is going on outside. By facing away from the center of the room and from one's roommate, one has fewer distractions and therefore can concentrate more effectively on school work.

*Undesirable placement.* There are several possibilities that one's study desk is improperly placed. If placed in front of a window, the distractions are numerous and often compelling. Also, the light may be entirely too intense at times, especially if one is working in direct sunlight. If the placement of the desk is such that it faces the center of the room or the door (which often may be left open), distractions are also numerous in that one has a tendency to look up each time someone passes the door or enters the room. The placement of study desks adjacent to each other so that the students sit face to face is also very poor. This arrangement is undesirable because the movements of another person are generally highly distracting. Then too, when people face each other, they are stimulated to converse frequently and this makes concentration on school work difficult, if not impossible.

Do the best that you can with regard to the placement of your study desk, and if it is still far from ideal because of factors beyond your control, emphasize other things discussed here that will improve your study environment.

## Keep a Businesslike Desk

*The cluttered desk.* Some people have no sense of orderliness. Their study desks are used as a catchall for everything from discarded clothing and empty boxes to old newspapers and outdated magazines. A desk so kept is certainly not conducive to effective study and learning. Save time and decrease your tension and emotion by establishing habits of orderliness.

*Have necessary equipment available.* One's desk top should be clear of all things except those immediately necessary for studying a given assignment. Textbooks, dictionary, and notebook should be arranged neatly at the back of the desk or in a bookrack at the side. Pencils, pen, eraser, paper, and other such necessities should be in a drawer where they can always be found easily. To establish habits of orderliness when they are not a part of one is often difficult, and only

FIGURE 38. A Properly Placed Study Table.

strong intention and much persistence can effect an improvement.

Establish the habit of orderliness with things, and it is possible that some of the habit will transfer to your thinking.

## PROPER LIGHTING

A factor essential to effective study that is often ignored by students is good lighting. Those students who do consider the problem generally concern themselves with only one of its aspects, namely, the *amount* of light. To secure proper light-

FIGURE 39. Improperly Placed Study Tables.

ing conditions when studying, several things must be considered.

## Daylight Versus Artificial Light

There is no substitute for daylight. Because daylight is white light (includes all hues) and because of its intensity, one is able to read with greater speed and efficiency and with

INDIRECT

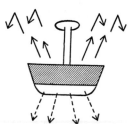

SEMI-INDIRECT

SEMI-DIRECT

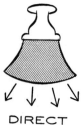

DIRECT

FIGURE 40. Four Types of Lighting.

less fatigue under daylight conditions than with any other type of light. This is one of the reasons for our earlier emphasis on the desirability of planning to do all of one's studying, or as much of it as possible, during daylight hours.

## Types of Lighting Equipment

The four types of lighting equipment (arranged in the order of declining effectiveness) in use are: indirect, semi-indirect, semi-direct, and direct. Indirect lighting provides reflected light—light that bounces back from the ceiling and walls. Indirect light is a diffused light because the rays bounce back from the reflecting surfaces in all directions. Hence, this type of light is *uniform* and there are *no shadows*. These are the two features that make indirect lighting so desirable.

A fixture that provides semi-indirect lighting allows some light to pass through a translucent shade directly to the student's working area, but most of it is reflected from the ceiling and walls of the room. In both of these types of lighting, the best reflecting surface is a light-colored, flat paint, with the ceiling being white, off-white, or light cream in color.

Semi-direct light is light radiated in all directions but through a translucent shade that diffuses the light somewhat and so reduces sharp shadows. Because much of this light falls directly on the student's working area, glare is common.

Direct light is the least satisfactory of all because it is directed downward by an opaque shade on one's working area from which it is reflected directly to one's eyes.

The decrease in acuity after reading for two or three hours under indirect lighting conditions is not much greater than when reading under daylight conditions; but the decrease in acuity when reading under the other conditions is very great, especially after three hours or more of reading.

## General Versus Local Illumination

Some students believe that the only area that needs to be illuminated is the immediate working area and that the rest of the room need be only dimly lighted. Such local lighting students often regard as cozy and private. This feeling may be characteristic, but coziness is not what you need especially since it does not make for more effective learning.

A combination of general and local illumination is recommended as most desirable. The general illumination of the indirect, diffused type eliminates annoying shadows and glare, and the somewhat more intense local, semi-indirect illumination (shaded with an opaque shade) on the working area provides sufficient light for reading.

Several highly lighted local areas, a condition resulting when several lamps are used in a room, is particularly objectionable because we have an almost irresistible tendency to look in the direction of these areas of high illumination. If there are several such areas, we move our eyes from one to the other and thus fail to concentrate on our work. Furthermore, when only local illumination is used and there is no general illumination, the contrasts in intensity of light in the various parts of the room are great. This means that as we look from one area to another our eyes must adjust constantly to the variations in intensity; since this is accomplished by the small muscles in the iris of the eye that fatigue easily, we experience considerable weariness and burning of the eyes. That these experiences have a depressing effect on our drive to study and our zeal to learn is obvious.

## The Amount of Light

The amount of light one needs or desires in a working area depends on a number of factors, such as, the amount of detail, the fineness of the work, the nature of the reflecting surfaces, and so forth. Psychologists and lighting engineers are not in complete agreement as to the number of foot-candles of light one should have for reading, but many indicate that 10 to 15 foot-candles is adequate for reading books and that 15 to 25 foot-candles is satisfactory for reading newspapers. Ferree and Rand [1] found that about one in four readers preferred the 10 to 15 range, only one in eight preferred less than 10 foot-candles, and four in 10 preferred more than 15.

## The Color of Light

Although sunlight contains all the wave lengths of the visible spectrum, the wave lengths that we are most sensitive to and that we use most in distinguishing details are the greens and yellows. The ordinary tungsten-filament lamp produces light that we see as yellowish, and that of the mercury-vapor arc lamp we see as bluish-green. Fluorescent lamps which are basically mercury-vapor lamps produce various hues depending on the materials with which the tubes are treated. In spite of these differences, experimental results indicate that visual efficiency is the same under mercury-vapor and tungsten-filament light. From the standpoint of providing optimum conditions for studying and learning, the color of the light is much less important than its intensity and distribution.

## Optimum Lighting for Studying

For best results, we find that the room in which one studies should be lighted with indirect lighting that eliminates shadows, contrasts in intensities, and glare. The study desk should be somewhat more highly illuminated, generally with 10 to 15 foot-candles of light diffused over the working area by a

---

[1] C. E. Ferree and G. Rand, "Good Working Conditions for Eyes," *Personnel J.*, 1936, *15*: 333–340.

lamp with a semi-indirect globe shaded with an opaque shade. The height of the lamp should be about 18 or 20 inches, so that the light is slightly above the eye level, and the lamp should be placed to one side of the work space so that one does not look directly into the light of the lamp.

FIGURE 41. Optimum Lighting for Studying.

Areas of high illumination in various parts of the room should be eliminated so as to avoid distraction and indirect glare. Surfaces in the working area should not be polished nor paper glazed since these produce glare.

If you observe these simple precautions, you will increase your reading efficiency and decrease visual fatigue. Do this and you will learn more with less effort.

## DISTRACTIONS

Anything that attracts our attention away from what we are doing is a distraction. What is a distraction for one person is not necessarily a distraction for another; and what is a distraction when we are doing one thing is not necessarily a distraction when we are doing something else. Some things attract our attention because of their strength, persistence, or particular quality; sometimes it is due to our own nature—our sensitivity, interests, and habits.

### Visual Distractions

We have already called attention to some of the visual distractions that one should eliminate when studying, such as marked contrasts in the intensity of illumination, glare, and shadows—particularly moving shadows.

Also, eliminate the visual distracters that many students keep on their desks or mounted on bulletin boards above them, such as pictures of intimate friends, mementos of formal parties, initiations, special dates, athletic events, and other exciting experiences. The illustration on the calendar on the wall, the view out the window, the letter from home on your desk, all can, and generally are, powerful distracters. Each of these stimuli arouses pleasant reminiscences with regard to the past or initiates daydreams with reference to the future.

Keep your study area free of such distractions. Place your study desk against a *blank* wall, as we have already suggested. Hang your bulletin board on a wall that is behind you when you are studying; keep photographs of friends out of sight on your dresser. Allow nothing in your field of vision when working at your desk except those things that suggest study.

## Auditory Distractions

Results of scientific studies on the effect of noise on studying, as such, are not available, but the implications found in laboratory studies and industrial experiments are suggestive for us.

Studies of typists working under conditions of quiet and of various types of noises indicate that the energy input is greater when working under noisy conditions, even though work output may be unaffected or but slightly affected. This is true of other skills also. The effect of noise on mental work, however, is generally such as to decrease one's efficiency.

The kinds of noises that are the most distracting are the interrupted noises because they constantly require us to readjust to them. A continuous sound that is high-pitched may also be very annoying because high pitches tend to cause pain. Sounds that are associated with fear, such as an unfamiliar buzzing sound, are also very distracting. We are particularly susceptible to the conversation of other people, especially when we do not hear distinctly what is being said. Are we missing something? Should we join the group? Such temptations as these are particularly strong when one finds the task at hand only moderately interesting or actually boring.

People differ considerably in their reaction to noise and other auditory distractions. Some people are capable of such intense concentration on a task that they shut out completely all distractions—they do not hear the noises. These people have a high level of tolerance for noise. On the other hand, many people are noise-prone; they react even to noises that most people ignore.

## Quiet as a Distracter

Absolute quiet is very oppressive and unpleasant for some people; hence, they find it very difficult to study in a quiet library. This is true when one is unaccustomed to quiet, just as noise is a distracter when one is not accustomed to it. Just as one can become adapted to noise and cease to attend to it (although not necessarily cease to respond to it), so one can become accustomed to quiet conditions also. From the standpoint of personal well-being, it is undoubtedly better to eliminate noise as much as possible and to learn to adjust to working under quiet conditions.

## People as Distracters

We are social beings and, therefore, derive much pleasure from being with others. For this reason, we seize every opportunity to be with others, to talk with them, and to participate in common activities. Since this tendency is strong in most of us, and since the presence of others readily releases this tendency, it is often very difficult to concentrate on academic work when other people are nearby. In fact, some people just cannot remain silent as long as another person is present—they just must keep the conversation going.

The best way to eliminate the distractions caused by people when one must study is to choose a working place where contact with other people is at a minimum. Some students solve this problem by hanging a sign on their dormitory door that reads, "Quiet! Genius at work!" When you are in the library, choose a place at a table where your back is turned to other students, or study in a cubicle provided for the purpose.

In any case, avoid facing the entrance to the reading room.

Decrease your opportunity for social contact when studying and you will thereby increase your concentration on your school work.

### The Pro's and Con's of Music

One cannot watch a television program and study at the same time. Nevertheless, some students try to do this daily. Obviously, their attention is divided, with most of it on the television program. This is not studying.

The situation is not quite the same when one studies with an accompaniment of radio or recorded music. One can study with quiet music as a part of the background because continued auditory stimulation generally is less compelling than visual stimulation. Some students develop such a need for a background of music when studying that it causes annoyance when not satisfied. As in the case of many things, this need for a background of music can be very compelling. When one establishes such a need, it is not that music facilitates learning and enables one to learn more with less effort, but that its absence hinders learning. Since such a need cannot be satisfied always, it seems the part of better judgment not to establish it in the first place.

Another reason some students like to have radio or recorded music as a part of the background when studying is that it is company—it satisfies their social desire and enhances their feeling of security. They do not feel so alone when they hear music and voices. Does the advantage of greater security outweigh the disadvantage of distraction caused by music? This is the question.

Some students reason that radio and recorded music enhance one's feeling of well-being and pleasantness, and that these are much more conducive to effective learning than depression and unpleasantness are. This is true, but the unfortunate implication in this view is that studying is necessarily unpleasant and depressing. This is certainly not true.

Perhaps the chief objection to music as background stimulation when one is studying is that one is very apt to follow rather consciously a familiar tune or radio announcements far oftener than one realizes, thereby dividing one's attention. Also, music is very apt to start a train of thought that is quite foreign to what one is studying. These objections to music are particularly significant when what one is studying requires considerable reasoning, comprehension, and memory for details.

## THE IMPORTANCE OF POSTURE

Attention implies some body tension; one cannot be relaxed completely and attend. One must assume a body posture that is conducive to attending well. This means that one should sit reasonably erect rather than slouch or assume body postures that suggest rest and relaxation. Certainly lying down on one's bed or bunk to read an assignment is the poorest thing one can do. This is especially true if one is accustomed to reading in bed before going to sleep, the purpose of which is to read oneself to sleep, a particularly easy thing to do when one is studying a textbook. Reclining when reading for relaxation is not particularly objectionable, but reading for the purpose of serious learning is a very different matter. You will learn best while sitting in such a position that indicates your readiness and willingness to work. *Avoid trying to combine rest and relaxation with studying,* for when you do you are most apt to end up resting.

# 9.

## *Prescription for Examination Jitters*

### TAKE THINGS AS THEY COME

**Remember Past Successes**

You have the leading role in the major dramatic production of the year. The final dress rehearsal is set for today. You gave your solemn promise that you will be there, and early. The play cannot go on without you. You cannot fail your dramatic coach. But alas! The weather! It has sleeted! Driving is not only hazardous, it is definitely dangerous. You live nearly three miles from the campus. Drive you must!

Under these circumstances, what do you do? Do you develop a sick headache, cry profusely, or go to bed and refuse to budge for three days? Do you blame the professor who set the date, or the weatherman whose prediction was correct, or go on a bender? Chances are you do none of these things. On the contrary, you view the situation as calmly as possible. Your attitude is: this is one of those situations that must be met. Although the hazardous drive will be neither pleasant nor easy, it cannot be avoided. Hence, you face it. *You face it because of your confidence in yourself.* Certainly, this trip will be a test of your skill as a driver and of your judgment in traffic situations. Nevertheless, you are confident that *you can meet this test successfully*.

## Life Is Full of Test Situations

Each time you participate in an intercollegiate debate, play a position on a team, sing a solo, lead a scout troop, preside as a class officer, ask for a date, or apply for a job, you are passing a test. In each case, it is a test of your ability to speak, to play, to sing, to lead, to preside, to charm, or to impress. Almost each day you meet a test in a traffic situation. A car comes seemingly from nowhere; you have little warning. You must make a decision quickly. You act. And you had better pass this test or it may be your final examination! Life is full of such tests.

Naturally, you have always thought of a test as of the academic type; you have associated examinations with school work. Perhaps you have even breathed a prayer that soon you will be graduated and so never again have to face another examination. If you have breathed such a prayer, you already know that it can never be answered. Tests and examinations are not found only in classrooms; they are a part of everyday life. Not only will you never be free of tests as long as you live, but you will have to meet many of them *without warning or notice*. Most of life's tests are of the "drop" type; they come without warning and without opportunity to prepare for them. Either you "deliver the goods" or you fail! As an active adolescent, or as an adult, you must expect to face several test situations each day no matter how long you live. Life is like that! Therefore, it is imperative that you learn early how to meet test situations. In this chapter we are concerned with learning how to meet one type of test situation—the academic type.

# ATTITUDES ARE IMPORTANT

## Be Concerned

Be concerned about meeting tests. It is normal to be concerned; it is even normal to have the jitters and to gripe a bit in anticipation of an examination. It is not only normal but also desirable, and if you are a typical man or woman, you do not find it difficult to adopt this attitude of concern. Past experience has taught you the necessity of looking after yourself, and you are in the habit of doing it. This habit of being concerned about your welfare and your future is a definite asset, and it indicates several things:

Concern indicates that you are somewhat tense. If this tension is moderate, it is a distinct advantage for tension makes you more alert and more eager to work. It gives you that "up-and-at-'em" zip that gets things done. It spurs you on to achieve your goal.

Concern also indicates that you are thinking, planning, preparing. If you are genuinely concerned about a forthcoming test or examination you will do something about meeting it, rather than depending on luck or magic to pull you through your hour of need.

Finally, being concerned means that you accept the challenge. You recognize that it will not be easy, but you are willing to put forth your best effort.

## Banish Worry

Worry is a crippling fear. When you worry you are very apt to sit, mope, and lament your fate, but you do nothing about the test you fear and dread to meet. Worry never solves any problems; it never spurs you on to achievement. On the contrary, it saps your energy; it paralyzes your thinking; it wrecks your morale. It makes you clutch at the false hope that somehow something will happen to save you from failure. Be assured, the only thing that will save you is intelligent effort systematically applied.

## Down Your Fear of Failure

The gods are on your side. Most people pass examinations —very few fail. If you have done all that you can to prepare adequately, why assume that you are bound to fail? Take courage! The very fact that you do will aid you to succeed more creditably.

If, after making a reasonable effort, you still fail, try to view your failure objectively. Try to discover the cause of your failure. Remember that the cause of your failure is usually more important than the fact of failure. Remind yourself that this is not your first failure nor will it be your last. Everyone fails in some things and at some time. You have failed to jump as high or as far as someone else, to run as fast, to play as skillfully, or to sing as melodiously. This did not stop you. You accepted your failure as an opportunity to review your technique, and then you pressed on toward your goal. Take the same attitude toward your academic failure. Make failure a stepping stone to new achievement.

## Don't Make Perfection Your Goal

No teacher expects you to write a perfect examination. In fact, a perfect paper is an inadequate measure of your knowledge of a subject. It merely indicates that you know all of the test, but how much more you know, which may be a great deal, is not revealed.

Suppose that you were given a mathematics test suitable to the third-grade level. Because of its simplicity, you could pass every item. Obviously, this test would be no measure of your knowledge of mathematics in that it would not be difficult enough. To measure your knowledge of mathematics adequately you must be given problems of such varying difficulty that you are able to solve some and not others. The true measure of your knowledge is in terms of the most difficult problems solved. If the examination is appropriate to your level of ability, you will fall short of perfection. This is as it should be.

The important thing, then, is that the examination gives you an opportunity to indicate the full extent of your knowledge. Therefore, do your best, but do not deplore the fact that you fall short of perfection. *Your measure is not found in a perfect score.*

## HOW TO PREPARE FOR EXAMINATIONS

### Prepare Adequately

Your first line of attack is adequate preparation. No examination or test situation can be met without it. Each time a surgeon is about to perform a major operation, he goes back to his medical books to refresh his memory on details of anatomy and techniques of surgery. He knows that his failure to meet the test may mean a life of misery or even death for his patient. He cannot fail! Hence, he does not rely on his memory of medical-school lectures. Instead he relearns the essential facts each time, just as he scrubs his hands each time. Such preparation strengthens his confidence in himself and gives him courage to face his task and his patient.

You too can face your tasks—your examinations—with courage and with confidence when you *prepare adequately*. Concentrate your time and energy on the acquisition of knowledge and the examination will take care of itself. The real test of your skill and efficiency as a student is in what you gain from conscientious and well-ordered study; the examination is merely the formal demonstration of this. Stress essentials. Banish examination jitters with adequate preparation.

## Face the Music

Admit that you do not hanker for tests or thrive on examinations. Most people do not. This, however, is no excuse for avoiding them or running away from them. Face them! Conquer them! Be master of the situation or it will master you. Draw strength from your past successes. Remember that this is not your first examination nor will it be your last. You have succeeded before, and, therefore, you should succeed more easily now.

You are not facing the music when you develop a psychological headache, a functional illness, or when you hibernate or get drunk. Nor are you facing the music when you allow yourself to become preoccupied with many inconsequential details in an effort to postpone serious study. Don't "kid yourself" by merely being busy. These things may be effective in keeping you from thinking about the examination, but they will do nothing to help you meet it—and meet it you must!

## Prepare Early

Anticipate your examinations by preparing for them early. By allowing yourself adequate time for preparation, you decrease your excessive tension and fear simply because there is little need for working under pressure. Leisurely learning gives you time to examine details and to absorb ideas. Effective, permanent learning is seldom done under marked pressure.

## Stress the Unfamiliar

Concentrate on those things which you do not know and which you understand less well. Beware of the false self-assurance that comes from knowing a *few* things well. The examination will cover the entire course. One safe trick does not win the game; one perfect answer does not pass the examination.

## Get a Panoramic View

See the course material in perspective. Note the major divisions and the subordinate parts. Grasp it as an organized whole. A jumble of disconnected and unrelated facts and ideas is of no more value to you than the several hundred disassembled parts of a typewriter thrown into a box. Details are of little value unless they are organized and integrated into a productive whole. Organized ideas produce results in an examination!

## Apply the Laws of Learning

Space your review periods; overlearn generously; recite often; read intelligently and with concentration; use several senses. Review these principles of effective learning, discussed in Chapters 4 and 5, before beginning preparation for an examination and use as many of these techniques as possible in your preparation. The purpose of a review is to *relearn* those facts and ideas you have partially forgotten; to *discover* those ideas that should have been learned in the past but were not; and to *integrate* effectively and meaningfully the material of the course so that it is seen in perspective and in its wholeness. To accomplish all this, you must use the best methods psychology has to offer. Take advantage of the offer!

## Find Out How You Will Be Tested

Most examinations are of the essay, short-answer, or objective type. Do you know the technique of meeting each most effectively? Ask your instructor which type of test or examination he will give. Knowing the type of examination you will be required to take will help you to prepare for it. If your instructor gives you sample questions, as some do, study them carefully with the view of becoming better acquainted with what the instructor may require of you, but do not expect that the examination questions will necessarily be chosen from the sample.

Adequate preparation, it is true, should enable one to pass any type of test or examination regardless of the type. Nevertheless, it is desirable to know how one will be tested. The reasons for this are several: When one knows how he is to be tested, he goes to the examination with greater self-assurance in that he knows what to expect. One is not caught by surprise nor does one have a feeling of being unprepared. It is very disturbing emotionally to go to an examination expecting an objective type of test only to learn that actually it is of the essay type. Knowing the type of test, one knows how to prepare for it. When it is of the objective type, one concentrates more on details and factual material; when it is of the essay type, one emphasizes generalizations more.

## Anticipate Test Questions

Put yourself into your instructor's place and try to anticipate the *specific questions* he will ask on the test or examination. This approach is particularly useful when the test is of the essay type. Having formulated quite a number of questions, write out the answer to each just as you would do during the actual examination period. Although this may, on first thought, strike you as a waste of time, it is anything but that. The psychology of this approach is that *you are prac-ticing doing the very thing you hope to do when you write the actual examination.*

The debater *practices* meeting questions likely to be asked during a rebuttal; he does not depend wholly on the inspiration of the moment. So also, you can *practice phrasing answers* to anticipated test questions so that when the time for answering them comes, you will be able to write complete answers skillfully phrased. Practice in answering test questions is just as essential to good performance as practice is for anything that you expect to do well. Is it any wonder that the answers to test questions often are so poor when so many of them are *first attempts?* You are seldom satisfied with your first attempt in other things, so why be satisfied with your first attempt in answering examination questions. Practice writing answers to anticipated test questions, and improve your skill in writing examinations and your grade.

## WRITING EXAMINATIONS

### Essay Examinations

When writing essay examinations, observe the following rules: Before writing, *read all the questions* through carefully. If you do not understand the meaning or implication of a certain question, or fail to appreciate the distinction between two questions, ask your instructor. He knows that you cannot demonstrate your knowledge unless you understand the questions. After you feel certain that you know the meaning of each question, *make brief notes on each.* This is advisable for two reasons. First, it gives you confidence that you know the material and that you will not omit essential points, due to forgetting, when you come to later questions. Second, it aids materially in organizing your ideas concerning each question. As a final preliminary to actual writing, budget your time. Do not expect to spend an equal amount of time on each question. Many instructors give more weight to some questions than to others. Beware of spending too much time on the first questions and too little on the last. Balance your time allotments so that you finish at or before the close of the examination period.

Now you are ready to begin writing the examination. Write legibly and neatly. Watch your grammar and your spelling. Make certain that sentences are complete. Avoid having too many or too few paragraphs. Strike a good balance between verbosity and brevity. Give some attention to style. Remember to *number points made* and to *underline significant words and phrases.*

Know what is asked for in each question and write to the point. Avoid disgorging all of your small store of knowledge in answer to a given question with the vain hope that the instructor will find among the chaff a few grains of information that really do pertain to the question asked. Be discriminating. Include only those ideas that develop a train of thought in logical fashion. Be assured that every instructor recognizes a student's limitations when the student undiscriminatingly enumerates ideas in serial fashion with little or no continuity.

Answer essay questions in the order in which the instructor lists them for his order may be purposive. If you prefer to answer some questions before others, allow sufficient space for the answers to the questions temporarily omitted. The instructor has a certain set when reading answers to test questions and if they are in an unexpected order, he may fail to give you credit for an answer given out of order. There is also the chance that the answer to a question may be omitted unintentionally when not answering them in order, and thus lowering one's grade substantially and without reason.

Be mindful of the instructor who must not only read your paper but 30, or 40, or 100 others. Make it easy and pleasant for him to read your paper and to follow your thinking. If an instructor must guess at what you write because he cannot read it, he is more apt to guess that it is wrong or that you do not know than he is to give you the benefit of the doubt. Do not take this chance!

### Short-Answer Tests

When writing in response to short-answer questions, be doubly certain to express ideas *briefly and exactly*. Choose your words carefully. Make each word count. Supplement statements with graphic figures, diagrams, formulas, simple graphs, and similar things that objectify ideas.

### Objective Examinations

When writing objective examinations of the true-false, multiple-choice, and matching or completion type, go through the test and mark all the items of which you are certain, then concentrate on those that require more thinking. If you have prepared adequately, you should be able to mark the majority of the items during the first reading. Knowing that you are certain of so large a number of items gives you confidence that you have done reasonably well on the test. Hence, any additional concentration on somewhat doubtful or difficult items serves to raise your score. This approach prevents the rise of the panic that is common when one encounters a number of difficult items at the beginning of the test and persists in thinking about them until they are answered. Not only does this approach usually result in rather marked emotion which hampers logical thinking, but it also results in a disproportionate amount of time spent on a few items.

Make certain that you read each item. Careless reading may result in skipping an easy item and so throw you for a loss on your score. In true and false items, look for the word or phrase that may make the statement true or false. In multiple-choice items, eliminate the possibilities that are most unlikely and reduce your choice to the two that appear most appropriate. In no case guess blindly; have a reason for your choice.

## SUNDRY SUGGESTIONS

### Learn by Doing

Remember that the technique of meeting an examination, like the technique used in any other skill, must be learned by doing. You can never learn it by running away from examinations or postponing them. Regard each test or examination as another opportunity to test your skill and ability to meet examinations. Practice with purpose and insight usually ends in mastery.

### Keep Fit

Sleep and eat regularly during examination periods. Spend a portion of each day in recreation or in some form of relaxation. Observe the rules of personal hygiene. Approach an examination as you would an athletic contest—physically fit. Efficiency in meeting an examination depends on clear, quick thinking and accurate recall. These are impossible when you are fatigued, sleepy, or hungry.

Every teacher has students who spend the whole night before an examination studying. In order to keep awake and at their task the whole night through, they drink quantities of strong coffee, apply cold packs to the head, and take pills that prevent sleep. The next morning, they go to the examination tired, sleepy, tremulous, and anxious, with the result that they cannot regurgitate what they gorged the night before. Not infrequently, such students leave the examining room without writing a single word—a total failure. These students assume that success depends on constant repetition. This is contrary to the laws of learning. Constant repetition results in a loss of attention and interest, and ultimately it leads to a disorganization of one's thinking and to actual forgetting of that which was previously known.

Keep fit. Learn to relax when face to face with an examination or test situation. Take it in your stride. Increase your chances of success; decrease the wear and tear on yourself.

### Shun Luck and Magic

Develop self-confidence; trust your knowledge. You know that a rabbit's foot or other good-luck charms cannot give you knowledge of science, mathematics, or history. Nor will crossing your fingers, as I have seen students do, keep you from writing the wrong answers in sociology, or the wrong endings in French or German. Stop being a primitive who lives by luck and magic. The atomic age requires reason and science.

### Act on Your Knowledge

Put the knowledge gained from studying this chapter to work. Adapt it to your own needs. Make the above suggestions so much a part of you that your approach to every examination will always be sound psychologically. *Conquer your examination jitters!*

# Appendix

## Projects and Exercises

In this appendix various projects and exercises are presented, under the several chapter headings, that are designed to direct your thinking and to aid you to establish the attitudes and techniques that make for efficient and effective learning. By carrying through to completion these projects and exercises, you will take the initial steps that ultimately will aid you to *learn more with less effort.*

## Chapter 1

*Exercise 1.*

*Purpose:* to stimulate thinking concerning common attitudes toward academic work and to lead the student to make a self-analysis of his own attitudes.

Divide the members of the class into a number of small groups or committees, of five to seven students each, with both sexes represented in each group (if the institution is coeducational). The members of each group are to elect their own chairman who is charged with the responsibility of facilitating, but not necessarily directing, the discussion carried on by the group. After the groups are organized, each group selects one question from the list of suggested questions given below, or one of their own choosing, which the group will discuss for 15 minutes. It is the duty of the chairman of each group to summarize and epitomize the discussion of his group. For the remainder of the class period, the chairmen of the several groups constitute a panel that presents and discusses the views and observations arrived at by the various groups, and invites the whole class to participate in a discussion of the findings.

## *Suggested Questions*

1. In what specific ways have your teachers tried to improve your learning techniques? Give advantages and disadvantages of each.
2. Why do some students resist and resent teachers' attempts to improve their learning techniques? Be specific in your answer.
3. How can one take a "new look" at the problem of academic learning? (See pages 4–6 for discussion.)
4. What approaches can one use that are acceptable to adolescents, that will lead them to accept new learning techniques?
5. Why do some adolescents resist change, and especially a change in study habits? Examine their psychology.
6. What type of teacher stimulates you to work the hardest in a course? The least?
7. Why do able students sometimes fail courses? Cite specific instances. What in your estimation were the causes of their failure?
8. What are the major causes of academic success? Of academic failure?
9. How can student-teacher relations be improved?

# Chapter 2

*Exercise 1.*

*Purpose:* to test the attitude of dependability toward one's work.

Attitudes are important factors in motivation. The kinds of attitudes one has often determine what one is motivated to do. Your attitude toward an academic subject or the instructor determines the extent to which you apply yourself when learning that subject. Are your attitudes such that your instructor is confident that you will apply yourself diligently? Can he depend on you to do your utmost?

Below is a list of 26 items, selected from a list of 200, that has been scaled to measure an attitude. Test yourself on this scale.

*Directions:* Read each item of the scale carefully and on a separate sheet of paper write down the numbers of the items with which *you agree.* We are chiefly interested in these items. Check a second time to make certain that you have recorded the numbers of all the items with which you agree.

## ATTITUDE SCALE [1]

1. One should stick to a job even if it is unpleasant.
2. Errors are permissible if one doesn't make too many of them.
3. Failure calls for another attempt.
4. An irresponsible person gets more joy out of life.
5. The path of least resistance is the best way.
6. One should always work to the best of his ability.
7. Although it is wrong to be late, it is sometimes necessary.

[1] Adapted from G. J. Dudycha, "A Scale for Measuring Attitude Toward Dependability," *Journal of Social Psychology,* 1941, *13*:59–69.

8. Only a weak-kneed individual gives up when faced with difficulty.

9. One isn't expected to complete all projects.

10. Only a fool is faithful in his work.

11. It does not pay to do more work than is assigned.

12. Routine work is usually easy.

13. Complete accuracy is imperative.

14. One should strive to be accurate but little mistakes do not matter.

15. One should always wait for instructions before beginning a task.

16. Persistence is not always necessary.

17. A daily routine makes work easier.

18. Varied speed of work is a sign of instability.

19. It doesn't make any difference if one is punctual or not.

20. Accuracy is necessary in important matters but not in unimportant ones.

21. It is better to work in spurts than according to a regular schedule.

22. Cheating frequently brings success.

23. If one does not succeed at first, there is no use trying.

24. A person should work regularly at some tasks but not at others.

25. One task should always be completed before another is started.

26. Persistence is not always rewarded by success.

Score the attitude scale by placing the scale value for each item with which you agree opposite the number of the statement. The scale values are given below. If you agree with an *odd number* of statements, the middle-score value is the measure of your attitude. If you agree with an *even number* of statements the average of the two middle-score values is the measure of your attitude. For example: if you agree with items 1, 3, 12, 17, and 25, the middle-scale value is 24, the scale value for item number 17. If you agree with items 3, 12, 17, and 25, then the middle two scale values are 18 and 24 (items 3 and 17) and, hence, your score is halfway between them, or 21.

Scale Values for the Attitude Scale

| Item | Value | Item | Value | Item | Value |
|---|---|---|---|---|---|
| 1. | 13 | 10. | 107 | 19. | 97 |
| 2. | 62 | 11. | 85 | 20. | 75 |
| 3. | 18 | 12. | 40 | 21. | 83 |
| 4. | 90 | 13. | 9 | 22. | 94 |
| 5. | 104 | 14. | 67 | 23. | 101 |
| 6. | 5 | 15. | 27 | 24. | 48 |
| 7. | 36 | 16. | 70 | 25. | 30 |
| 8. | 16 | 17. | 24 | 26. | 55 |
| 9. | 79 | 18. | 56 | | |

Interpret your score by comparing it with the table given below which indicates the degree of your attitude toward dependability.

Table of Scale Values

| | |
|---|---|
| 5–24 | Very dependable |
| 27–40 | Dependable |
| 48–62 | Average |
| 67–83 | Undependable |
| 85–107 | Very undependable |

*Exercise 2.*

*Purpose:* to evaluate your study habits and attitudes.

Respond to any one of the following study habits inventories, each of which is designed for college freshmen: *Survey of Study Habits and Attitudes, Wrenn Study Habits Inventory,* The Psychological Corporation, 522 Fifth Avenue, New York 36, N.Y.; *Spitzer Study Skills Test,* World Book Company, Yonkers-on-Hudson, New York; *The College In-*

*ventory of Academic Adjustment,* Western Psychological Services, 10655 Santa Monica Boulevard, West Los Angeles 25, California.

*Exercise 3.*

*Purpose:* to evaluate your interests with the view of increasing academic success.

Interest is an important determiner of academic success. In the case of required subjects, concerning which there is no choice, one must develop the greatest degree of interest in these subjects possible; in the case of elective subjects, however, one can choose according to one's interests. As a means of discovering more adequately the nature of your interest pattern, mark one of the following interest tests. The results will aid you in making an intelligent selection from among the elective subjects offered. *Interest Index,* Educational Testing Service, 20 Nassau Street, Princeton, N.J.; *Vocational Interest Analysis,* California Test Bureau, 5916 Hollywood Boulevard, Los Angeles 28, California.

## Chapter 3

*Exercise 1.*

*Purpose:* to observe the characteristics of trial-and-error learning.

Give a key ring containing a dozen or more keys to one of your fellow students and ask him to find the key that unlocks a given lock. Watch carefully his method of attack. After he has found the correct key, take the key ring from him and manipulate the keys in such a way that he loses track of the right key. Then, hand the key ring back to him and have him find the correct key again. Do this a number of times until he is able to identify the correct key almost immediately. Observe carefully the way in which he apparently learns to find and recognize the key.

Now that he has learned this simple task, ask him to state how he learned to identify the correct key. Record both his introspections and your observations. Repeat the experiment with several different people so that individual differences are evident.

You may substitute a mechanical puzzle of some kind (the bent nails that must be separated, etc.) for the keys, if such is available.

*Exercise 2.*

*Purpose:* to demonstrate retroactive inhibition in recall.

In this experiment you will learn to substitute letters for digits. The letters to be substituted for the digits 1 to 0 are given below as *order A:*

Order A:    1 2 3 4 5 6 7 8 9 0
            T D R B P F N H L J

When the signal to begin working is given, start by writing 10 as TJ, 11 as TT, 12 as TD, 20 as DJ, 21 as DT, and so on. Continue writing as fast as you can until time is called, which will be at the end of three minutes.

Immediately after time is called, take a second sheet of paper and repeat what you just did, except with a different set of letters given in *order B:*

Order B:    1 2 3 4 5 6 7 8 9 0
            S A X C U K M G E Y

Continue writing these symbols for 90 seconds. When time is called, write the letters used in *order A,* or as many as you can, in order from 1 to 0 without referring to the sequence given in the book. Record the number of symbols you are able to remember correctly.

The following class period, take another sheet of paper and repeat the experiment but use the letters given in *order C:*

Order C:    1  2  3  4  5  6  7  8  9  0
            W  I  H  M  A  C  V  R  T  D

Immediately after time is called at the end of three minutes, start copying on another sheet of paper several paragraphs from your text. Continue doing this until time is
called at the end of 90 seconds. Immediately after time is
called, write the letters used in *order C,* or as many as you
can, in order from 1 to 0. Record your results and compare
with those obtained when using the letters of *order A* during
the previous class period. You should have recalled more
letters correctly for *order C* than for *order A* because of the
retroactive effect of learning *order B* immediately after learning *order A.*

Report your results to your instructor, who will tabulate
them for the whole class and report the results for the entire
group.

## Chapter 4

*Exercise 1.*

*Purpose:* to compare the results of spaced and unspaced
learning.

Select the telephone numbers of 15 faculty members [2] and
list them in a column with the name of each person opposite
each number. Read through this list of telephone numbers as
many times as necessary, at *one sitting,* for you to be able to
remember the telephone number of each person. Tally each
reading so that you have an accurate check on the total
number of readings necessary for perfect reproduction.

Test yourself for accuracy after 24 hours and record the
number of telephone numbers remembered correctly.

Two days after the original learning, select another list of
15 telephone numbers of local businesses whose numbers you

[2] All the members of the class should use the same list of numbers.

do not now know but do have some need for. Be sure that these numbers are like those of the first list in length and complexity. Read through this list of telephone numbers and corresponding names *three times in succession* (no more, no less) at 12-hour intervals, as 7:00 A.M. and 7:00 P.M., for example, until you know the list perfectly. Record the total number of readings necessary for mastery.

Test yourself for accuracy again 24 hours after the last reading and record the number of telephone numbers remembered correctly. Now compare the number of readings necessary and the number of telephone numbers accurately recalled after 24 hours when the unspaced method of learning was used with the corresponding results when the spaced method was used.

Report your results to your instructor, who will tabulate them for the whole class and report the results for the entire group.

*Exercise 2.*

*Purpose:* to discover the value of verbalization as an aid to learning.

Perform the experiment discussed on pages 93–95 of this book. Study the graphs in Figure 22 for *one minute,* then close your book and try to reproduce the graphs from memory. After you have included as many details as possible, return to Figure 22 and study it by *describing,* for one minute, what you see. Say as many things about the graph as you can. Then take another sheet of paper and reproduce the figure a second time from memory. Compare the two figures you have drawn for completeness and detail, and note how much more you know about the graphs after verbalizing about them.

Repeat the experiment with another person as the subject

and you as the experimenter. Note carefully the differences in your subject's learning when the two approaches are used. Write out your observations.

*Exercise 3.*

*Purpose:* to observe the value of using several senses when learning.

Select some learning material that you have had an opportunity to learn in the past, but had not learned too well, and apply the procedure of using *several senses* when learning it now. You may select a 200-mile highway route that you have traveled a number of times but never learned the names of all the towns, in order, through which you passed. Or you may take a schematic drawing of a famous battlefield that you once studied in history. Or you may select a poem or prose selection, or some such material, that you once learned partially.

If you choose to learn the highway route, *say aloud* what you *see* when you are looking at the road map; note how what you say *sounds* when you say it, and *draw* the route and *write* in the names of the cities and towns and the route numbers.

Repeat the experiment with someone else as your subject. First allow him several minutes (depending on the nature of the material) to study the material in his own way. Then have him tell you what he remembers, as you record the things he recalls. Follow this by another period of study of like length during which you emphasize that he not only see the material, but that he talk about it, hear what he says and that he draw or write what he is experiencing. At the close of this second period of study have him report again to you on what he now remembers. Note how much more was gained the second time than the first. Write out your conclusions.

*Exercise 4.*

*Purpose:* to observe the value of using immediate goals when learning.

For the next week, in all of your school subjects, set specific and immediate goals when preparing each assignment or part of an assignment. Write out or outline a detailed plan for the whole day in which you plan specifically either how much time will be allotted to a specific task or portion of an assignment, or set specific quotas as to how much you will do before stopping work. Carry this plan through with determination and without exception.

Note the satisfaction that you experience each time one of those immediate goals is achieved, and how the psychology of immediate goals works to spur you on toward further achievement.

At the close of each day check off the goals that you have achieved and note how many things you have accomplished by setting immediate goals. Take a few minutes to write an introspective report on your accomplishment and to evaluate the effectiveness of the method.

Continue this practice long enough to establish firmly the habit of setting immediate goals, and then you will follow the practice rather automatically. Also, continue writing your brief, daily, introspective reports on the effectiveness of this method and you will soon find that you are learning more with less effort!

## Chapter 5

*Exercise 1.*

*Purpose:* to observe the value of recitation when learning.

Select some prose selection or poem that has considerable imagery in it and memorize it with emphasis on *recitation*. A number of the Psalms in the Bible (1st, 8th, 23rd, 29th) can be used as learning material if you have not memorized them previously.

When memorizing your chosen selection, do three things:

1. *Read* the entire selection *aloud* several times.
2. *Draw pictures* (using stick figures) that represent the imagery contained in the selection. Put the whole selection into pictures. Remember that your *imagery* is far more important than the quality of your drawings, and that you are trying to *objectify ideas,* not produce art.
3. *Write* out the selection.

The purpose of this exercise is to force you to *do a number of different things* with what you are learning. The value of these learning techniques comes in the *doing*.

Write an introspective report describing your experience while learning this selection. State specific ways in which meaningful associations were discovered as a result of *oral reading, drawing* and *writing*.

*Exercise 2.*

*Purpose:* to observe the value of overlearning.

Return to the material used in Exercise 1 of Chapter 4. Review the two lists of telephone numbers just enough times so that you can give each number in each list correctly. Now select one of the lists (all the members of the class better select the same one) and overlearn it by: (1) *repeating* the numbers in the list; (2) *writing* the numbers; (3) *dialing* them, without raising the receiver. Do each of these *three times a day for one week*. This may seem unnecessary, but persist in doing it to demonstrate to yourself the value of overlearning.

At the end of the period of overlearning, reproduce both lists of telephone numbers and check those in both lists of which you are doubtful. Check both lists for errors and make a record of both your accuracy and certainty with regard to each list. Without further practice of either list, reproduce both lists after one month and record both your accuracy and certainty with regard to the numbers of each list.

These two testing periods can be done during class periods and the results for the group summarized and reported.

*Exercise 3.*

*Purpose:* to observe the value of different mental sets when reading, and the value of marking one's text.

Read through Chapters 4 and 5 using the following systematic plan:

1. Read through the two chapters at your usual speed without pausing if you do not understand some things fully. During this reading, look for the general plan of the chapter, the main topics covered, and the various aspects of each learning technique presented. Get a *broad view* of the techniques of efficient learning.

2. Reread each chapter after a rest pause of several hours, but with a *different purpose.* This time, read the chapter *with emphasis on the various divisions and subdivisions.* Reread a part or a whole section that is not clear to you, before going on to another section. *Underline* crucial words and phrases. *Write* brief comments into the margins that will summarize points. *Number* the points made with regard to each technique. Make each chapter yours by doing something specific with it. *Personalize these chapters by putting something of yourself into each.*

3. Return to these chapters for a third, quick, but meaningful reading after another rest pause. Your purpose this

time differs again from the other two. Read with the intention of *summarizing, integrating, and seeing the material in perspective.* This reading should not take much time. You should confine yourself to reading topic sentences, the underlined words and phrases, and your marginal notations.

Now that you have followed the above procedure diligently, write out your reaction to this method of studying. Note specifically your confidence that you know the material covered.

## Chapter 6

*Exercise 1.*

*Purpose:* to observe progress in learning a skill.

Select some skill for observation that you are now learning. Some suggested skills are: typing, archery, tennis, golf, swimming, gymnastic skills (on the horse, buck, parallel bars), operating some type of machine, or other such skill. You will be wise to select a skill that you are just beginning to establish rather than one that is partly established and that you are seeking to perfect. Starting with a new skill has the advantage of giving you the opportunity to observe all the stages in its establishment.

To begin this experiment, first list all the points made in the subdivisions of this chapter under the heading "Aids and Techniques," and become thoroughly familiar with each. After you become familiar with the possible aids, *outline a method of attack* on the skill you are learning that will enable you to use as many of these aids as possible. Keep this outline available so that you can refer to it often.

Next make a thorough study of the section of this chapter entitled "Progress Made in Learning Skills," so that you know what to look for as you progress in the establishment of your skill.

Each day you practice your skill according to your outline, write out an introspective report that will include a statement of the nature and extent of your progress for that day, along with your observations on the subjective aspects of your experience. If the skill you are establishing affords any objective measures of accomplishment, record these daily also. File each of these reports with the outline of your method of attack. After you achieve a fair degree of skill in that which you are learning, review all of your introspective reports and the objective measures of progress you recorded and write an evaluation of the overall progress you made in establishing the skill.

## Chapter 7

*Exercise 1.*

*Purpose:* to evaluate class attitudes and behavior and to gain insight into personal motivation.

Write a careful and honest analysis of the behavior and attitudes that are characteristic of you in a particular class of which you are now a member. Indicate as fairly and honestly as you can the *reasons* for your attitudes and behavior. Include in your evaluation comments on such matters as these: How well do you like the course? What are the specific reasons for your liking or not liking the course? What feelings or emotions do you experience when attending the class? Does the period generally seem long or short? Why did you take the course? Can you distinguish between your attitude toward the course and toward the instructor? Where do you sit in the classroom and why? How do you participate in the class activities and how often? Compare and contrast yourself with the instructor. How are you alike and how different? What would you like to do or say in this class that you do not do? How do you evaluate your own performance in the class?

Do not confine your comments to answering these suggestive questions; rather, give a full and frank evaluation of your relationship to the particular course.

## *Exercise 2.*

*Purpose:* to obtain an evaluation of personality characteristics of importance to academic success.

Mark the *Edwards Personal Preference Schedule* [3] which gives data concerning 15 personality traits. Score this test and convert the scores into percentile ratings. Your instructor will give you a list of the traits measured and help you interpret your percentile ratings. Make a profile of your percentile scores so that you can see readily in which traits you are strong, average, or weak.

## *Exercise 3.*

*Purpose:* to relate measured personality characteristics to personally recognized attitudes and behavior.

Reread your evaluation of your attitudes and behavior made in Exercise 1 and try to gain insight into the reasons for these attitudes and this behavior in terms of the personality traits measured in Exercise 2.

## Chapter 8

## *Exercise 1.*

*Purpose:* to make a time schedule for the week.

Following the suggestions given in this chapter, make a time schedule for the week taking care to include all essentials and to evaluate realistically the time necessary for each task.

[3] The Psychological Corporation, 522 Fifth Avenue, New York 36, N.Y.

*Exercise 2.*

*Purpose:* to examine your room arrangement from the standpoint of effective study.

Draw to scale a floor plan of your room and draw all the furniture in the room as it now is. Then, draw one or more floor plans to scale that will incorporate the various principles discussed in this chapter. Indicate which plan, in your estimation, incorporates the largest number of principles to best advantage.

*Exercise 3.*

*Purpose:* to examine the lighting in your room.

Write a report listing the desirable and undesirable aspects of the lighting in your room. State specific ways in which the lighting can be improved so that it complies with the recommendations given in this chapter. If you have an exposure meter that measures light in foot-candles, measure the amount of light you have in various parts of the room as well as on your study table. Indicate these readings on your floor plan.

*Exercise 4.*

*Purpose:* to examine the distractions experienced in your room when studying.

List the various distractions experienced over a period of several days and find ways in which they can be eliminated or decreased.

# INDEX

Abstracts, use of, 131–132
Accuracy, learning skills and, 160–161
Aggression, reaction to forced learning, 29–30
  toward others, 30–33
  toward things, 33
  treatment of, 30, 32–33
Amoeba, 50, 51
Aptitude, interests and, 42
Attention, learning and, 78–79
  skills and, 143–144
Attitude, academic success and, 163–164
  change in, 4–6
  indicated by class behavior, 167–170
  interests and, 42–43
  knowledge versus learning, 26–28
  mature, 164–165
  nature of, 162–163
  scale for dependability, 221–222
  toward learning, 6–7
  toward learning skills, 137–140
Attitudes, reasons for poor, 170–172
  toward examinations, 208–210

Baruch, Dorothy W., 32
Behavior, modification of, 55–56
Book, W. F., 145

Bryan, W. L., 144, 145

Change, reaction to, 7–11
  resistance to, 13–16
Concept formation, 70–71
Conditioning, interest and, 45–46
  use of, 46
Coöperation, means of, 177–179
Cramming, 85

Dallenbach, K. M., 76
Desk, placement of, 192–193
  study, 192–194
Distraction, 201–205
  auditory, 202–203
  music as, 204–205
  people as, 203–204
  quiet as, 203
  visual, 201–202
Distributed learning, 85–89
Distributed practice, length of practice periods, 154
  length of rest periods, 155
  reading and, 123–124
  skills and, 153–155
Dudycha, G. J., 67, 68, 126, 221
Dvorak, A., 160

Emotion, learning and, 78
Examinations, attitude toward, 208–210
  frequency of, 207